BLACK WATER

BLACK WATER

WATER

Family, Legacy, and Blood Memory

DAVID A. ROBERTSON

HARPER PERENNIAL

Published by Harper Perennial, an imprint of HarperCollins Publishers Ltd

First published by HarperCollins Publishers Ltd in a hardcover edition: 2020
This Perennial trade paperback edition: 2021

HarperCollins books may be purchased for educational, business, or
sales promotional use through our Special Markets Department.

HarperCollins Publishers Ltd
Bay Adelaide Centre, East Tower
22 Adelaide Street West, 41st Floor
Toronto, Ontario, Canada
M5H 4E3

www.harpercollins.ca

Map on page ix by Scott B. Henderson

All photos are from the author's personal collection.

Library and Archives Canada Cataloguing in Publication

Title: Black Water : family, legacy, and blood memory / David A. Robertson.
Names: Robertson, David, 1977- author.
Identifiers: Canadiana 20210238291 | ISBN 9781443457781 (softcover)
Subjects: LCSH: Robertson, David, 1977- | LCSH: Robertson, Don, 1935-2019. |
LCSH: Fathers and sons. | LCSH: Indigenous peoples—Manitoba—Biography. |
CSH: Authors, Canadian (English)—21st century—Biography. |
LCGFT: Autobiographies. | LCGFT: Biographies.
Classification: LCC PS8585.O32115 Z46 2021 | DDC 971.2004/9732300922—dc23

Printed and bound in the United States of America

LSC/H 9 8 7 6 5 4 3 2

For Dad

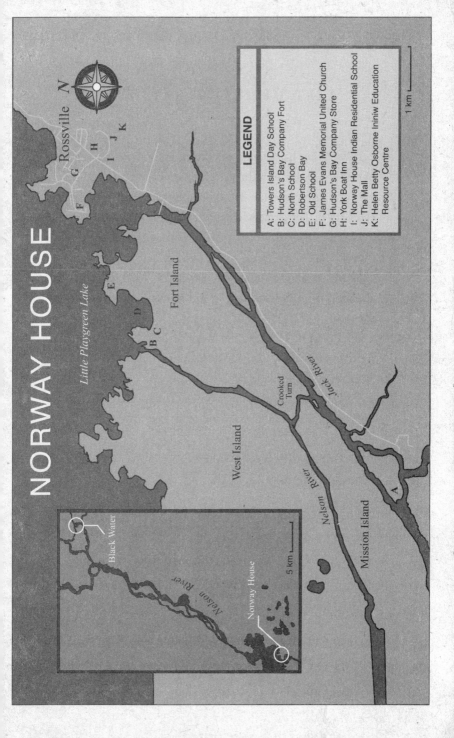

NORWAY HOUSE

Rossville N

Little Playgreen Lake

Fort Island

West Island

Mission Island

Crooked Turn

Nelson River

Jack River

LEGEND

A: Towers Island Day School
B: Hudson's Bay Company Fort
C: North School
D: Robertson Bay
E: Old School
F: James Evans Memorial United Church
G: Hudson's Bay Company Store
H: York Boat Inn
I: Norway House Indian Residential School
J: The Mall
K: Helen Betty Osborne Ininiw Education
   Resource Centre

1 km

Black Water

Nelson River

Norway House

5 km

LIST OF ILLUSTRATIONS

BLACK WATER

PROLOGUE

D ad and I are sitting at a café by my work. He's ordered an Earl Grey tea with some sweetener. I have a decaf coffee splashed with almond milk. I'm facing Dad and a mirror, and I trade glances between him and my reflection, wondering where the years have gone. I'm growing my hair out, and all I can see are the grey strands. I tease my wife, Jill (who is Métis), that I'm aiming for a man bun, but really I think I'm trying to connect with something that I've been working hard to understand since I was in my late teens. That is, what it means to be Cree. I guess I feel as if long hair would make me more Indigenous. Growing up, I had this vision of what an "Indian" is, and like it or not, that vision, despite all the work I've done, has stayed with me. In reality, a lot of my Indigenous friends have braided hair and a lot have short hair. It's a good thing my hair grows so damn slow; I've got time to figure out if I'm bugging Jill or trying to be cultural.

That's the thing about journeys: they're never really over. I'll probably be doing this when I'm Dad's age. Maybe I won't be deconstructing the reasons why I'm growing out my hair, but it will have something to do with identity. It will have something to do with what it means to be Cree.

My dad is Donald Alexander Robertson—Dulas, to those in our home community, Norway House Cree Nation. He's got an easy way about him, always has, but it's nothing to do with his eighty-two years. Everything he does is purposeful and measured. For a middle-aged guy living with anxiety, I find comfort in the way he exudes calmness. It's in the way he talks; Dad says something only when he believes he has something important to say. He's thoughtful and deliberate. I've learned to be patient in speaking with him, to watch his eyes, which are smaller than they appear behind prescription lenses, while they search for the right words. And then to listen carefully, because he won't repeat himself. I've learned through practice, because conversations with Dad aren't new. We've been at it for a while, and often have sprawling discussions that somehow lead us into a better recognition of ourselves. The café is a frequent setting for our talks, but they don't exclusively occur here—there's also the golf course, the car, Mom and Dad's house, a restaurant both of us can eat at (I'm vegan, and he's got no large intestine), or before the lights dim in a movie theatre.

At the café, Dad gives me most of his attention, except when a friend walks by, which isn't uncommon. He used to run the place I work at now, the Manitoba First Nations Education Resource Centre (MFNERC), in the early 2000s and still knows people there. He likes to have coffee with me, then see his pals. He roams the hallways with his easy stride and seeks people out. He's got a laugh that echoes through the building—you know when he's around—and it's infectious. People say that Dad and I have the same laugh. People say that Dad and I have the same walk. If you looked quickly at a picture of Dad's basketball team at Cook Christian Training School in the mid-1950s, you'd think that I'd pulled a Marty McFly and was standing there in his place. I like that we have these similarities.

We've been having these conversations for almost thirty years. I'll ask Dad a question about his life, referencing any period between 1935, the year of his birth, and now. He'll think about it over a sip of Earl Grey tea, then respond. It'll be either the most thoughtful answer you can imagine, one that feels as though he's prepared for it (and he very likely has), or utterly dismissive, disappointing, because I want to know more, because I expect more or at least something different.

"You know," he said to me recently, "you can't tell my story from my perspective. This is your story, even if it's about me. It has to be that way."

His story. My story. I'm not sure it's that simple. It's our story, and whether it's about a time in his life or a time in mine, what I want—what I've always wanted—is to figure out how his life, my life, and our relationship have shaped who I am.

Time has moved quickly for me as well as for Dad. I notice this when we talk. Sometimes it feels like looking at him is another sort of mirror altogether. Not just because we walk the same or laugh the same. I see in him things I want to be at the age of eighty-two, and things I do not want to be, because of the choices I think he made and how they affected me—even though I can't, even though I wouldn't, change what has happened. That's confusing for me, but it's a reality I've come to accept, even embrace.

From what I understand, Dad, a broad-shouldered, tall Cree, and Mom, English, Irish, and Scottish, with a beautiful smile and flowing brown hair, chose not to raise me and my brothers as Cree to keep us from the difficulties they thought we might face growing up in Winnipeg as First Nations kids. I don't think Cam and Mike even knew they were Indigenous—I certainly didn't, and we never talked about it. Not with Mom and Dad, not with each other.

"What do you regret most?" I once asked Dad in the car on the way home from an afternoon at our local golf course.

"That I didn't teach you the language," he responded. Which I interpreted as: "I didn't teach you about who you are."

There are times when I catch myself staring at him and comparing the Dad I have in my life now with the other versions I knew growing up. If I knew him at all. His job was always a mystery, and I never asked about it. So, too, was his home community, Norway House. I didn't hear about it until I was a teenager. When I spent time with him, I was just happy to see him. We didn't have the kind of talks then that we do now. We used to golf on the weekends. We used to go to movies. But I never thought he'd be the best man at my wedding. I never thought he'd sit with me over coffee and answer all the dizzying questions I threw his way, mindfully stirring sweetener into his tea, thinking of things to say to satisfy my curiosity. Expected or unexpected, disappointing or mundane.

I watch his veins shift with each movement of his hand, the protruding tendons dance under his weathered brown skin. I watch his hand and think about his life, and the lives of those who came before him. About my paternal grandmother, Sarah Robertson. I called her Nana. That's one of the only things I can remember about my grandmother: what I called her. The rest of my memories of her are just images. She's sitting in the kitchen in her house somewhere off Osborne Street, wearing a flowered dress, her arms outstretched and ready to receive me, ready for me to run across the room and collide with her. It's like she's a dream I had once.

Dad and I haven't yet started our dance of questions and answers today. Since he knocked on my office window and we ambled over to the café, we've talked about the weather, how Mom's doing, how my kids are doing, how he's doing, how I'm doing. He's wearing navy-blue slacks that work hard to hide the boniness of his legs but fail, Hush Puppies on his feet, a white T-shirt underneath a black V-neck sweater, a fall jacket even though it's late summer. He gets cold easily. He looks contemplative; his eyes are narrowed, eyebrows collapsed, sending wrinkles across his forehead. When his eyebrows are relaxed, the lines remain. I have those, too, like him.

"What are you thinking?" I take a sip of coffee, then place it back onto the table.

We meet eyes. There's four feet of air between us. We're in the least intimate setting, but I've never felt closer to him. He's absently playing with the lid of his tea, then leans forward the smallest distance.

I hear him breathe.

"I want to go to my trapline one last time," he says.

I cannot breathe.

I know he hasn't been to his trapline for almost seven decades. We've been on a journey as father and son for thirty years, and for the first time, it feels like we've found our destination. And I think, "Maybe we've been headed there all this time." Whatever truths exist between us, the end of our journey is in front of us.

My dad is in his early eighties, and despite my best efforts to will his immortality, he's not getting younger. He will not be a boy again. He will not be the father I used to know—the father I was unfamiliar with—again. Years from now, he will not be this father either. Years from now, he will exist in memories, and I will be left to collide with the open arms of those moments.

"Okay," I say. "Let's go."

After all this time, I think we're ready.

PĒYAK (ONE)

Winter had passed slowly. The days grew shorter but somehow seemed longer. It didn't help that it had been, even by Winnipeg's lofty standards, a particularly cold season. Some days felt frozen in time, as if tomorrow would stubbornly refuse to come. It was like Christmas when I was a child. My impatience led to eternal sleepless nights in the bedroom I shared with Mike, wondering what the morning would bring. The morning always came. Mike and I would rush out to find a plate of cookie crumbs, an empty glass of milk, and whatever action figure we'd asked Santa for. The morning always came, so did the summer, and so did today.

I'm sitting in the lobby at Perimeter Airlines, on a chair beside the Elder's couch, in anticipation of Dad's arrival. He's uncharacteristically late. He arrives everywhere at least fifteen minutes early, and I've always been the same way. It's not that I'm afraid he'll be a no-show. We've been planning this trip for a year, and I know how excited he is for it, even though you wouldn't know it by looking at him. It's that I'm about to hurtle into the throes of panic, a state I'm all too familiar with. He calms me, and I need him to be here.

I noticed it while driving—a near indescribable elevation in my chest that then coursed through the rest of my body. I felt hot. My limbs were trembling, and my heart began to race, beat heavy.

There were no parking spots when I arrived. Of course there weren't. It was cosmically predetermined that I'd have to walk from the overflow parking to the terminal, because when my anxiety is bad, I can barely stand up, let alone walk a block with a backpack and a carry-on suitcase. But I made myself do it, walk the distance, and now I'm here. That's how you have to deal with the devil on your shoulder. When it says you can't do something, you have to do it anyway. Tell it to fuck off. We have conversations, anxiety and I. They aren't as pleasant as the ones I have with Dad, but they can feel as important.

Across from me, there's a mother and a toddler who seem to be waiting for our same plane. It'll stop in Cross Lake First Nation before continuing on to Norway House, a short fifteen-minute flight between the two communities. All at the same time, the mother's scrambling with luggage and toys, fishing a wipe out of her purse because the kid's got some ketchup on his cheek, and keeping an eye on him, making sure he doesn't bother the strange man who, unbeknownst to anybody, is having a panic attack.

"It's okay," I tell her.

I don't mind the kid bumping into me as he plays, scattering his toys all over the place, jumping from chair to chair, pretending the floor is lava. How could his mother know that I have five kids of my own, and this sort of thing, this small taste of a child's particular brand of anarchy, is not a bother at all? I don't mind the kid bumping into me not only because I've experienced it a thousand times before, but also because watching him and his mother is a distraction. Distractions are good when you're having a panic attack, but on this occasion, it's still not enough. Sometimes the devil on your shoulder doesn't give a shit if you try to ignore it.

Dad isn't here yet. I hold off as long as I can, not wanting to deal with anxiety in the way that has always made me feel weak. But eventually, I thrust a hand into my backpack and search, with unsteady fingers, for medication. I chastise myself for feeling this way. I've gotten better at accepting the fact that sometimes anxiety will just happen without warning. A static shock. But because of where I'm going, and with whom, I don't understand why. Why today? I want to feel normal. I want to feel enthusiastic without impediment for what lies ahead.

I've been waiting for this moment for so long—before I knew I was waiting for anything, before I knew where our decades-long journey would take us. I've been waiting for this moment since before I'd even heard of Norway House or Black Water, the trapline where we're headed. I've been waiting for this moment since before Dad got sick, almost twenty years ago. I've been waiting for this moment since before my dad moved out. I've been waiting in the moments I've held, and the moments I've lost, since I was a toddler, like the child bumping into me now, jumping from chair to chair. I've been waiting to find out who, and why, I am, and those answers are closer than they've ever been.

MOM AND DAD never told me that I was Indigenous when I was a kid, and because of that, I grew up disconnected from that part of my identity. I often felt confused about who I was; I only knew that I was different—that I looked different, and sometimes I was treated different. But I didn't know why, just how it made me feel. I remember so desperately wanting to be liked but thinking, at the same time, that there was nothing likeable about me. I've always been sure this low self-esteem was related to an incomplete sense of self. I've always been equally sure that my parents made an intentional choice not to tell me about my indigeneity, in consideration of the time in which my brothers and I were born. The world that Dad, in particular, knew we would grow up in. This choice was reflected in other decisions Mom and Dad made, like moving to River Heights, a Winnipeg neighbourhood that was predominantly white, where only one self-identified Indigenous family lived. (Not us.)

I've not one recollection of meeting or knowing of another Indigenous kid in any of the schools I attended, from Brock Corydon Elementary to Kelvin High School. At the age of thirty-three, I found out that a friend I'd known since nursery school was Métis, but like me, she wasn't told she was Indigenous until she was older. I learned about my background in junior high school, although I don't remember how I found this out—I just know that kids started to ask if I was an Indian, and something must have clicked. But what was an Indigenous kid who's disconnected from his culture to do? If somebody asked, I denied it. I had no desire to be Indigenous because everything I'd learned about Indigenous People during my formative years was negative.

In high school, my favourite accessory was a Cleveland Indians hat. I was hiding behind the Indians' grinning mascot, Chief Wahoo. If I was making fun of myself, my classmates wouldn't make fun of me, right? I'd beat them to it. If there were jokes about Indians—and there were—I'd laugh along. If questions arose about my heritage, I lied. Why would I want anybody to know that I was an Indian? My friends watched the same movies I did: non-Indigenous actors with the right skin tone (or the right bronzing agent), wearing headbands to keep black wigs in place, acted like savages needing to be tamed. My friends cheered for the same sports teams. I didn't own the only Chief Wahoo hat in my school, and everybody knew the signature move of the Atlanta Braves: the Tomahawk Chop. We had the same news channels showing criminals who were usually "Aboriginal in appearance." We read the same comics. I was educated by ignorance, by the perpetuation of stereotypes through popular culture, by the wilful denial of colonial history in the classroom. History told with tunnel vision.

My parents couldn't have known the impact their decision would have on me, and I can speak only for myself, not my brothers. They've come to their own identities, and the impact of my parents' decision is different for them than it was for me. They no doubt look back on their lives in a way that is unique to each of them, just as our Cree identity is unique to each of us. I know the impact of my parents' decision only with the benefit of hindsight, with enough adult knowledge to see through the influence of those negative stereotypes and my narrow view of a people and community of which I was a part. I can look back on my life, on Dad's life, and see how both the good and the bad experiences eventually led us to Black Water.

FOR THE FIRST three years of my life, I lived in Brandon, Manitoba, with my parents and my brothers, in a modest rented bungalow in the northeast area of the city. The only thing I can remember about this time is playing in a carport awash in green light. I look at the cracked concrete, at my clothing, my skin, my hands, and everything is green. Then I look up, see the green polycarbonate roofing with the sun shining through, and the mystery is solved.

I'm still not sure where I was. My parents don't even agree. I asked both of them on separate occasions. Dad told me the carport belonged to the Gregorys, who were our neighbours. Mom thought it was the people next door to the Gregorys. She said, as well, that I would've been too young to remember something like that. I must've played in the carport when I was older, she said, and we were visiting. She might be right. Dad might be right. They both thought they were right. Memories are funny that way—they can be different in two people's minds, but true to both.

Two types of memories shadow us: integral moments in our lives—ones that shape who we are or who we'll become, for better or for worse—and others that just seem to hang around, blissfully unaware of their insignificance. But maybe because of this endurance, these other memories are not insignificant at all. We just don't know what they mean yet. All I know is that *my* truth is playing atop cracked concrete with green covering everything: the concrete, my toys, an old barbecue, my body. I'm submerged in that algae-coloured image, the only one I have from my time in Brandon. Playing under polycarbonate carport roofing, rotating my hands as though I've never seen them before.

When I was three years old, we moved to Winnipeg, into a white bungalow with red trim that had two trees in the front yard, one on the left of the walk and one on the right. The tree on the left was, and remains, an incredible climbing tree. It had a swinging branch that extended out across the walk. When I was a teenager, that branch claimed a friend of mine as its first and only victim when he ran to catch a Frisbee in the middle of the night and struck his forehead against the branch in full stride. This prompted its removal, even though it wasn't the branch's fault. Minutes later, that friend ran into a hedge while chasing the same Frisbee. The tree on the right had several thin reddish trunks that extended from the ground, creating a small space at the centre that we sometimes pretended was a jail or a hiding place. The tree was unclimbable but still a haven.

There were three bedrooms. Mom had one to herself after she and Dad separated, Cam had another, and Mike and I shared the last. Although we each had our own twin bed, we would often end up together at night, with a flashlight, reading comics until Mom caught us. Once she left the room, we did it all over again. Comics were a big part of our lives. We used to take our allowance and walk to Styx Comics, at Corydon Avenue and Lanark Street. We'd buy superhero comics and read them, conspiratorially, deep into the night. We also loved action figures and would create fortresses for them by bunching up our comforters into towering shapes. The great thing about creating fortresses this way is that it creates a new stronghold every time.

CAMERON, MY ELDEST brother, is five years older than me. When I was a child, he was, as one might expect, both my hero and my tormenter, fulfilling the role of older brother perfectly. His exploits are legendary, at least to Mike and me—like the time he forced me to drink out of the toilet after swearing he'd peed in it (he hadn't, but as I think about it now, it's still pretty gross). Or when he made Mike sit in a tub of ice-cold water. While he performed his tormenting duties admirably, we could also depend on him for anything we needed, and he protected us fiercely. When I was bullied by a kid my age, Cam put a stop to it. When I was bullied by a classmate of Cam's, somebody about the size of Shrek, he did the same. He loved me far more than he tormented me. He included me in his friendship circle when he didn't have to (they called me Little Cam). And it was Cam, later in life, who stayed on the phone with me when I was having a panic attack in the middle of the workday, then drove across the city to be at my side. But Cam didn't walk to Styx with Mike and me every Saturday, allowance in hand, excited to pick up the latest issue of *The Amazing Spider-Man* or *The Avengers*. Cam didn't play with action figures in our makeshift fortresses either. Mom once told me he'd never played with toys. I think that he always seemed older than his age because he had to be. After my parents separated, he was the man of the house.

THE FIRST MEMORY I have from the Queenston Street bungalow is a microcosm of my early years. I'm wearing a yellow long-sleeved turtleneck underneath denim overalls and running at full speed down the hallway, away from my bedroom towards the living room. I don't know what I'm running from; it's very likely Cameron. I take a sharp right turn from the hallway into the living room, not daring to look behind me, and there is Mom. She's sitting on the couch, absolutely proper, as she's always been. (The compliment I hear most about my mother, aside from the fact that she's beautiful, is that she's a "lady.") When she sees me, she doesn't look startled because she doesn't want to startle me. She doesn't flinch. She doesn't look behind me. She opens her arms and I run into them. There is nowhere safer in the entire world.

Mom has been there every step of the way for all three of us boys. She raised us single-handedly after my parents' separation, which happened soon after we arrived in Winnipeg and lasted for a decade. During those years, we saw Dad only on the weekends. He loved us and he loved Mom, but Mom was pretty much it for us. Sometimes I picture myself walking to Styx with Mike, ready to buy superhero comics and never realizing there was a superhero in our house all along. I didn't recognize it back then. We were kids. I do now. She was a single mom raising three boys, and I think most people would agree that we turned out okay. My brothers and I grew up close, and we have remained close over the years. This was important to Mom. She wanted us to be able to rely on each other. We have. We can. Even now, with all of us living busy lives and together raising eleven children, if one of us needs the others, we're there. That's because of her too.

I WENT TO Brock Corydon Elementary School, named in honour of Sir Isaac Brock. Built in the 1950s, it's a traditional brick-and-mortar building with a field where we used to play Red Rover during recess. South of the school, there's a larger field where I played soccer, and across from that, there used to be a hockey rink. I spent countless hours playing shinny there—from when it opened right up until the floodlights shut down—freezing my toes and sipping hot chocolate made for us by Bob, the rink attendant.

My third-grade class had an abundance of Davids—three, to be exact. Because of this, each David became associated with the first letter of his last name: David K., David D., and David R. If I bump into somebody from Brock Corydon today, I'm still called David R. Our third-grade teacher, Diane Ratuski, was one of those people you always remember because of the influence they had on you. My kindergarten teacher, Mrs. Halas, was also like that. Mrs. Halas had Do-Do Bird, a hand puppet that she used in class to help engage the kids. Ms. Ratuski introduced me to writing.

Recently I was rooting through the School Day Treasures book that Mom kept, and in the grade three section, I found a book I'd written in March 1986 called *Tarts for Jack*. It's dedicated to my girlfriend (she's unnamed on the acknowledgements page, and I can't remember who this was) and is about a boy named Jack who isn't allowed to eat tarts his mother baked. He devises a plan to steal them but is unsuccessful. "I had an urge for tarts, Mom. I'm sorry," Jack laments after crashing to the floor. He'd tried to reach them on top of the cabinet by using a stool.

The About the Author page reads: "David Robertson is 9 years old and he lives in Manitoba. He loves writing books. He wrote four books this year. His favourite hobby is art & gymnastics."

He loves writing books. Ms. Ratuski helped me create *Tarts for Jack* and the three other books I wrote during the 1985–86 school year. The one I remember most is not *Jack*. I'd forgotten all about that book—along with my girlfriend, and the fact that my favourite hobby was gymnastics (although I do have a fourth-place pommel-horse ribbon that makes more sense now). Instead, the one I remember most is *The Bestest Poems I've Ever Sawed*.

Ms. Ratuski had us write poetry. To my knowledge, this was the first time I'd ever written in the form. The rest of my classmates worked at their desks, but for some reason, I decided to do my writing in the closet, and was allowed to. I shoved jackets and boots and backpacks out of the way, flattened my foolscap against the floor, and got to work with a chewed-up pencil. (Another thing I found in Mom's School Day Treasures is an envelope labelled "David's Pencil." It was broken into three pieces and annihilated by teeth marks.)

You wash all up
Until you're clean
And then you'll look like
A girl attraction machine.

Ms. Ratuski took those poems, typed them up on whatever word-processing software there was on the Commodore 64 (I want to say WordPerfect?), printed them out, and stapled the pages together into a book. I remember holding that book in my hands, and the flood of emotions that followed. Through all of those emotions came a singular thought. After school that day, I raced across the field, past the hockey rink, through Brock-Fleet Park, down Queenston Street, and into my house.

"Mom!" I shouted. "I want to be a writer!"

My exact words were that I wanted to be a *world-famous* writer. Mom didn't respond by telling me that getting published was too hard, or that in Canada, writers typically don't earn enough money to make a living. She didn't tell me to dream a little smaller. She said two simple words that I have carried with me ever since: you can. Many people have played a role in giving me the privilege and the platform to do what I do. Ms. Ratuski was one, but Mom had the biggest influence.

She's been there. For all the seemingly mundane experiences in life—the ones we take for granted but miss the most when time goes by—as well as for the highlights that stand out. Cam and Mike have been there too. Their presence in my life is a movie I can replay in my mind.

Cam spreading lettuce, a stand-in for rotten seaweed, all over my bedroom floor the evening I finished reading *Night Shift* by Stephen King, then jumping out of the partially open closet after I got in bed because he knew how much the boogeyman scared me. Cam coming to watch me play house league hockey at River Heights Community Centre, with me doing my best to impress him, looking at him each time I did something good just to make sure he'd seen it. Making comics with Mike in the dining room and trying to draw as well as he does, or playing at Brock-Fleet Park, hiding from each other in the bushes around the perimeter of the playground. And Mom, sitting on the couch in the living room, her arms outstretched, waiting for me to run into them.

I have fleeting images of Dad, moments that beg for context. There's Dad in a kitchen. We boys are sitting in various positions around the kitchen table. I'm in a high chair, I think. It might've been in Brandon, maybe Calgary. The point, I suppose, is that he's there. He's got a shag hairstyle like Austin Powers. He's holding a new electric razor against his face, pretending to give himself a shave, pretending that a Cree guy needs an electric razor at all. There's Dad pulling away from the curb with Cam and Mike in the back seat. I'm crying. My arms are folded up like a Murphy bed, resting on the windowsill, as I try to hide my anger and sadness. My chin's on my arms and I'm watching them leave without me, not understanding why I can't go to *Return of the Jedi* too. There's Dad at Cottonwood Golf Course, a twenty-seven-hole course consisting of a blue, white, and red 9 (easiest to hardest, in that order). The red holes were a beast. They were short but treacherous. There was too much water, and they had too many dogleg lefts for a right-handed kid with a slice. Everybody, including Dad, jockeyed for a round of 18 on the blue and white. I can picture us golfing there, a tract of land just off the Trans-Canada

Highway, about forty-five minutes east of Winnipeg. I'm wearing a red windbreaker and using Dad's old Wilson clubs. He's got on a golf shirt from one of the Indigenous organizations where he's worked (which meant nothing to me at the time) and a baseball hat. He used to look ridiculous in a baseball hat (Mom would say he still does). Strini Reddy, one of Dad's oldest friends, is there with us. That's where I knew Dad best, where I felt closest to him as a kid. It was our time, and we didn't have much of it. I think I still like golf, even though I'm awful at it, because it reminds me of Dad, of when I was young and with him. It was our *Return of the Jedi*.

Mom and Dad couldn't have known how their decade-long separation would compound my cultural disconnect. They couldn't have known that even if they'd decided to tell me about my Cree heritage, to raise me as an Indigenous kid, Dad wouldn't have been around enough to follow through. Mom's always been there, but she wasn't equipped to do that job; she had enough on her plate. Her presence, the presence of my brothers, the absence of my dad—all had a profound impact on me. What I knew about myself and what I did not.

NĪSO (TWO)

I don't want anybody to see what I'm doing, so I sit by the Elder's couch in the lobby of Perimeter Airlines, with the child bumping into me every few seconds, both hands inside my backpack, blindly trying to get the lid off my Xanax. If you're having a panic attack, childproof lids present an obstacle not unlike opening a wine bottle when you've misplaced the corkscrew, so it's an eternity before I'm able to slip a pill into my mouth. Soon after, the sliding doors open and Dad saunters in. He walks past the Chicken Delight towards the service counter, and somewhere between there and here, he sees me. He puts his index finger up—"Just a sec"—and checks in.

I wait some more, wondering if he was able to tell, in the moment we met eyes, how I'm feeling. Generally, people can't. If you look at me when I'm having an anxiety attack, you'll never know that I feel wretched in body and mind. I've learned to hide it, put on a front, ignore it as best I can. It's really only Jill who can tell. She says it's in my voice: a slight crack, something razor thin.

Dad sits down on the chair beside me, not the Elder's couch. He's got a navy baseball cap on and has doubled down on the fall jacket by layering up with two of them, anticipating cooler days in Norway House. I say nothing about the anxiety attack, now churning below the surface of my skin in a slow boil. His presence relaxes me almost more than the pill I placed on my tongue.

"You ready?" I ask, managing a smile.

"I'm ready," he says.

Dad and I and the other passengers are each given a newspaper and a pair of earplugs when we board. The earplugs are warranted; small planes make a ferocious buzzing sound while in the air. Luckily, we aren't flying in a torpedo-shaped plane, like the one I used to take to Opaskwayak Cree Nation while doing work there years earlier; it was so miniature in scale I almost had to crawl to my seat. Still, the space is limited here, especially for a six-foot-four guy (Dad's shrinking in his age but still pushing five ten). Dad likes his space. We sit across the aisle from each other.

The city disappears against the horizon, and in its place appears the patchwork quilt of the prairie landscape, which in turn gives way to the lush green embrace of the boreal forest with its watery veins. I pass time alternating between looking out the window and seeing if Dad is doing better with his crossword puzzle than I am with mine. This is the competitive nature of our relationship, although I'm not certain Dad's trying to out-crossword me. This competitiveness is more typically borne out in our golf games (where, it should be mentioned, I have yet to beat him, except once when he was sick, and though I'd like to count that as a victory, I can't in good conscience). The one-sided crossword competition is a dead heat, and it remains that way as we land in Cross Lake First Nation, where we wait for several minutes while passengers, including the child and mother from the airport, disembark.

The closer we get to Norway House, a place where Dad hasn't lived for over sixty years, the less he works on his crossword and the more he stares out the window. I spend less time on my crossword, too, but instead of staring out the window, I watch Dad. I wonder what he's looking at, what he's thinking about. Maybe he sees his trapline, nestled protectively within the tributaries below, arms swaddling the earth. The place where he and his family used to hunt, snare, and fish to make a living. Maybe he's remembering the path he used to take with his family to get from one community to the other, and the series of waterfalls they had to navigate. Or maybe, or maybe, or maybe. What I do know is that I see a look of peace on his face, in his eyes, that I haven't seen before, as comfortably as he walks and talks and goes about his life. I think about my own anxiety. I feel calm, and I know it's more than just the pills. Dad's going home. I'm going home too.

THE FIRST TIME I visited the community, years earlier, it felt familiar to me, even though I'd never been there before. An Elder told me during the trip that the feeling of familiarity was called blood memory, and that Norway House, as well as the water and trees surrounding it, had always been a part of me. I met the Chief and told him how much I liked his jacket, a royal-blue fall coat with a red lining and the community emblem on the left breast. I asked him where I could get one. I wanted to take a piece of

Norway House back with me when the trip was over. Without hesitation, he took off the jacket, placed it on my shoulders, and said, "Welcome home." I understand now that the piece I wanted to take back with me was always there, and it always will be. Black Water is no different.

This is not to take anything away from Winnipeg. It's been home to me since I was a child. At this point, I don't think I'll live anywhere else. We've got roots here, my wife and I. People we can't leave, won't leave. Her parents, mine. Her brother, my brothers. Our nieces and nephews. But I've got roots in Norway House too. Cousins, an aunt and uncle. More tangible—though not more real—than blood memory. There's only one other place that carries the same sense of belonging, the same feeling of home: Melita. But I'm conflicted about that. Because while Dad and Mom met there when he was the town's United Church minister, while so many of the seminal moments of my youth were spent there, while I have roots there as surely as I do in Winnipeg and Norway House, Melita is also the place where I first experienced racism.

WHEN I WAS a boy, Kathleen Eyers, my maternal grandmother, sometimes used to give me cash, maybe five dollars, to get a treat. I'd run from her house on Ash Street, across the back lane, between the Royal Bank and the movie theatre, south down Main Street, past the barbershop and pool hall, beyond the municipality office, and into the drugstore. There was a magazine stand right beside the cashier. I used to spin it around to look at all the comics until I found the perfect one. Spider-Man. The Avengers. Superman. G.I. Joe. Firestorm. It's one of the many clear memories I have of my time in Melita.

Mom, Mike, Cam, and I used to go there for Christmas and two weeks every summer. We'd pile into Mom's Pontiac Acadian—Cam in the front, me and Mike in the back—and make the four-hour trip to southwest Manitoba. It doesn't seem that far now—I've driven to both the West Coast and the East Coast with my family—but back then, those hours felt like an eternity.

One of my favourite graphic novels is *This One Summer* by Mariko Tamaki and Jillian Tamaki. It's a coming-of-age story about a girl's emotional awakening at a cottage she's been going to every summer all her life. The life-changing experiences Rose has over the course of this beautifully written and illustrated book are familiar to me because they remind me of the time I spent in Melita as a kid. So many firsts happened there—so many lasting moments imprinted themselves on my mind like remembered dreams and helped shape me.

Past the museum, across the playground, on the other side of the field from Grandma and Grandpa's place and the Presbyterian church, in a two-storey brick house, under the stairs on the first floor, I had my first kiss. One of those sweet, full-lip kisses you see in movies like *My Girl* (only without the killer bees). The girl's name was Melanie, and for a few years, she was one of the reasons I looked forward to my time in Melita each summer. We used to play in the park together, shoot arrows in the front yard of her house at a target attached to a tree, and do all the things there were to do for small kids in a small town. Then one year, I arrived in Melita to find Melanie going with (a 1960s term seems appropriate here) a blond-haired, blue-eyed kid from town. I remember seeing them together while sitting atop a sloped tin roof attached to the Presbyterian church. By the next year, she'd moved away.

I suffered my first broken heart in Melita, and as it turned out, my first broken bone. It happened during an ill-advised

game called Kill the Carrier that I played with my brothers and
our cousin Shayne. If it sounds awful, it was. One person would
punt a football to an awaiting player, the carrier, who was typically stationed in front of Grandpa's garage. The carrier would
then have to run with the football across the field, get past three
tacklers, and make it to Ash Street. There was only one rule: you
couldn't wuss out. My injury actually occurred when I was a
tackler. Cam was the carrier, and he received the ball and charged
towards us. The carrier was supposed to *evade* the tacklers, but
Cam just kept running at me. I talked to Mike about the incident last year. He said, "You were not good at that game. To
avoid contact, you usually went limp before someone got close."
He wasn't sure why I panicked that night and ran instead. Not
towards Cam, but away from him. "I'm just surprised you didn't
turtle. One of the great mysteries." Cam followed me like a bull
and slammed into me, and I fell backwards onto my arm. Within
the hour, I was at Melita Health Centre getting a cast. The doctor called it a greenstick fracture. Cam had broken my arm, but
he was also the first person to sign my cast. I think that says a lot
about him.

It's a wonder I didn't break something when I drove a car for
the first time, under Shayne's supervision, on the back roads of
Melita, in Auntie Joan's light brown Mercury Cougar. I was, at
most, thirteen years old. Shayne taught me how to handle gravel
roads by encouraging me to go fast when the car started hydro-
planing. "Never hit the brake," he cautioned. "Just ease your foot
off the gas, and if the car's going right, turn the wheel right."
I'm not sure how great a teacher he was; I didn't get my driver's
licence until I was nineteen.

I drank a beer for the first time with Shayne, too, at a party
outside town. I remember sitting on a couch with a bunch of

older kids, sipping on a cold one, feeling about as cool as I'd ever felt. Labatt Blue, if memory serves.

The first time I played golf was at the Melita club. Grandma used to get me a summer membership when I visited as a child. Despite its diabolical layout of hills and winding fairways, the course remains my favourite. It was more the company I kept that made it special. It was my mom's sister, Auntie Joan, and how she tossed her still-smouldering cigarette onto the ground before every shot. She had a distinctive waggle, a little touch of grace. After the shot, after a whispered curse under her breath, she'd pick up the smoke and keep sucking away at it. It was Shayne and his specially made driver for his specially developed swing—a violent, John Daly–esque lash. Shayne, always trying to drive the first green, never quite making it, but never giving up. And it was Grandpa, teaching me how to be calm, to resist slamming my club against the ground after I'd hit a bad shot, because I couldn't go back and change what had already happened. Grandpa never swore after he hit a bad shot (I never heard him swear my entire life); instead, he'd mutter, "Christmas!"

Great-grandma Jobbins lived in a pink bungalow on Maple Street north of Summit, a short walk from Grandma and Grandpa's house. I used to spend a lot of time there. She had a porcelain bowl of multicoloured mint candies waiting for us on her coffee table. We ate those candies and played cards. Rummy. She cheated. Badly. She peeked at what cards the people to her right and left had, then played her own hand based on the information she'd gleaned.

One morning, as she lay with her husband, beside whom she had slept for decades, she didn't wake up. It was 1988.

Her funeral was held at the Presbyterian church across the yard from Grandma and Grandpa's place. There was a viewing prior to the service. I stood in front of her casket and put my hand on her hands, which were crossed over her body. She looked and felt like a wax figure. Cold and smooth to the touch. I watched Great-grandpa Jobbins do the same thing, touching her cold cheek with his warm hand, before his knees buckled and he collapsed to the floor, sobbing.

I have all these memories of my great-grandma, even though she lived hundreds of miles away from me. I can smell her house. I can taste her mints. I can see all the porcelain knick-knacks she kept. Her elephant collection. I can picture her eyes peeking out from behind her cards to check out some-body else's hand. I have memories of her death, of her funeral, of saying "Cheers!" at the reception in the basement of another church on Main Street because I was a kid and didn't know any better. And I wonder why I've no memories like this of Nana. Sarah Robertson, Dad's mom. I wish I did, even just the smell of her. Something more than that one image of her in a flow-ered dress. Nana died in 1985, only three years before Great-grandma Jobbins, but I have not one memory of her funeral. Was I even there?

MELITA'S POPULATION HAS hovered around eleven hundred people for as long as I can remember. It used to be printed right there on the sign when you entered town. But for the last ten years, the population has been slowly, albeit steadily, dwindling. Reaching desperately for eleven hundred, but falling towards a thousand. The average age is forty-five—older than the median age in Canada—which fits how I've described the community in the past: an agricultural retirement town. And like Winnipeg's River Heights, like the schools I attended growing up, Melita is predominantly white. I asked Shayne about this recently—if he remembered any diverse people in the town in the 1980s. (He lives in Alberta now.) "When I was growing up, there were only two Black kids. One was two or three grades higher than I was, and one was in our grade," he explain.ed. "And there were a couple of Chinese kids, from the family who owned the Chinese restaurant. That's it."

Built to the west of a bend in the Souris River, Melita is in the province's banana belt, an area that's warmer than the rest of the region. When I was a kid, watching the classic Manitoba weather channel with its beautiful red-and-green screen, the town was often the hotspot. In recent years, Melita has embraced the whole banana belt thing as a tourist attraction. There's a huge banana mascot across the street from the old hotel, right near the mini-golf course, and yes, if you're wondering, the banana is wearing a belt.

For me, the attraction is not a large banana with a weird smiley face, but that the town exists somewhere outside of reality. When you turn onto Boundary Street and drive into Melita, it feels as though you're entering a time in history when nobody was a stranger. You wave at everybody you pass while driving—just put your index and middle fingers up without letting go of the steering wheel. You don't lock your front door at night. You don't lock your car either. And every day at 9:00 a.m., 12:00 p.m., 1:00 p.m., 6:00 p.m., and 9:00 p.m., the siren affixed to the fire station behind Grandma and Grandpa's house goes off, signifying the time to be at work or school, lunch, back to work or school, supper, and curfew. Or at least it used to be that way, until the siren broke down a couple of years ago.

"Do you remember me ever knowing that I was Indigenous?" I asked Shayne.

He took a moment, then responded thoughtfully, "I think you knew you were different."

I've never been entirely sure when knowing I was different turned into knowing I was Indigenous. I've examined my school photos, from kindergarten to grade twelve, and I think I seemed very Cree. I even asked my friend and fellow writer, Jen Storm, an Anishinaabekwe, for backup on this.

"I mean, I was obviously Cree, right?"

She laughed. "*So* Cree."

The thing is, I wouldn't have known what that looked like back then. My only image of an "Indian" came from comic books or sports team logos or settler history lessons. In one of my favourite comics, *The Fury of Firestorm* #1, the antagonist is named Black Bison. The issue is an origin story for the villain, and what you get at the end of it all is an angry Indian hell-bent on revenge against white people. He's dressed in hide pants, mukluks, and a bison head, and of course, he's bare-chested. His weapons are a staff and shield with feathers all over them, and he rides a reanimated stuffed horse. I would've had a picture like *that* in my mind and developed a sense of what it felt like to be associated with it from the way people treated me. Because, simply, I had dark skin and black hair. Shayne was right. I knew I was different. Most of the time I was able to pass as non-Indigenous, but sometimes I wasn't.

BESIDE THE MELITA & Area Arena, overlooking the golf course, is the town pool. It has been renovated and renamed the Melita Aquatic Centre, but during my childhood, the pool was relatively small, rectangular in shape, and surrounded by a white chain-link fence with just enough grass for families to set up camp with all the necessities of a day-long excursion: towels, coolers, beach umbrellas, pool noodles. I remember the water being an impossibly perfect shade of blue.

In any pool, you are completely exposed. It's just you and your bathing suit. If I knew that I was different, as Shayne said, this knowledge assuredly came from moments like this: standing in a crowd of Melitans at the pool on a hot summer day with my dark brown skin in an otherwise white crowd.

One hot afternoon in the banana belt, a red-headed kid started chasing me around the pool, threatening to beat the crap out of me. All I could think to do was run—and wonder why the kid wanted to beat me up in the first place. I hadn't done anything to him. I hadn't looked at him funny. I hadn't said one word to him. But there he was, this kid with fiery red hair, the size of André the Giant, hot on my tail, fists raised, full of a mysterious anger that matched the colour of his sunburnt skin. It wasn't until he started calling out, "Burnt toast! Burnt toast!" that I understood why he'd taken an interest in me. Dark brown skin. Burnt-toast skin.

Fortunately, it was an advantage to be scrawny. The kid, built like a tree trunk, couldn't catch me no matter how long he chased me. Around the pool, through the obstacle course of pool-goers and their paraphernalia, and into the Aqua Velva water, holding my breath to stay hidden, the only place in town where I looked like everybody else. This memory of being chased is as vivid as the one of playing underneath the poly-carbonate carport roofing, awash in green light, when I was a toddler in Brandon. He never caught me, but I think he did something worse and more lasting.

If that kid was going to treat me like that just because of my skin colour, then I didn't want to look that way. I didn't want to

be different. This is not me ruminating in hindsight. I know that
I felt this way as young as the age of eight or nine. I know
that this feeling of not wanting to be myself started in Melita.
Despite this, I hold fond memories of the town and my time
spent there. When I've gone back to visit my grandparents at the
cemetery, there have been peaceful moments I've cherished. I
love small towns. I love spending time in Norway House, and I
love spending time in Melita. It's more than just having strong
roots in both places; it's the feeling of calm, of peace, that I rel-
ish. That's why I'm conflicted about Mom's hometown, a place
where I've always felt at home. For every good memory—sitting
in a darkened basement with Grandpa near the end of his life and
holding his bony hand in a thunderstorm—there is, and always
will be, burnt toast.

Auntie Joan worked as the administrator for the Rural Municipality of Arthur, the region that included Melita and neighbour-
ing communities. Soon after the burnt-toast incident, I was riding
along in her Mercury Cougar while she checked road signs inside
and outside of town to see if any were damaged or missing.

I turned to her and asked, "Why is my skin different? Why is
it so ugly?"

She pulled the car over.

"David," she said, "people would die to have skin like yours.
It's not something you should be ashamed of. You should be
proud of it."

I didn't believe her.

NISTO (THREE)

Norway House Cree Nation appears on the horizon, then we're soaring above it towards the airstrip, the community laid out before us. I see the Helen Betty Osborne Ininiw Education Resource Centre, a K–12 school on the northeast edge of the reserve, with its donut-shaped main building and four wings that reach out towards the surrounding terrain. It is one of the largest First Nations schools in Canada. To the right, past the mall and council office, there's the York Boat Inn, where Dad and I are staying tonight. The hotel was new on my first visit eighteen years ago, and from other visits, I know that nothing much about it has changed: the dark green flooring, the leather couch and vending machine in the lobby, the rooms that require actual keys and not key cards. From the plane's oval window, I watch the sun's light glitter across the surface of Little Playgreen Lake, a large body of water on the west shore of the community.

There's a stark contrast between this side of the lake and the other. On the north shore you find the school, the mall, the hotel, the arena, and many prefab houses built close together in an urban-like sensibility. Referred to as Rossville, this is where the majority of people live on reserve. The area Dad and I are flying over now, to the south, is closer to what you might expect on reserve: dense forested land sporadically populated with houses in various states of repair. It might take you a few minutes or more to walk from one dwelling to another, and looking down at them now, I'm reminded of notes I'd made in a pink Hilroy scribbler on my first trip: "There are no street addresses here; instead there are landmarks. A broken-down Ford with flat tires. A peculiar-looking tree that distinguishes itself. An unoccupied red tricycle. A man carving a shoe out of a wooden block. I bet people give directions like 'Oh, Joe's place? It's the one with the trampoline out front.'"

We make our descent. The airplane wobbles gracefully towards the landing strip. Neither Dad nor I finish the crossword puzzle; Dad didn't look at his again once we'd taken off from Cross Lake. He'd been taking in the view, and perhaps considering, as I am, the intimate relationship between the community and the land and the waters. How linked they are, but how, too, this living arrangement is utterly and implicitly respected by Indigenous People, both in Norway House and across Turtle Island, because we understand this relationship isn't co-dependent. The land and the water need nothing from us, and we need everything from them. Even in this moment, as Dad and I navigate the narrow steps that lead us from the airplane to the tarmac and solid ground, I'm reminded of that.

The airport, the landing strip, is surrounded by impenetrable green woods, as is the entire community, and I wonder if that's what really makes this place feel so much like home to me. The forest, the water. If that's the case, and I think it is, then tomorrow is the real homecoming. For Dad. For me. Today is just another step on our journey. A journey that started—really started—when I was just a confused kid fighting his way through junior high.

MOM'S STORAGE ROOM is a treasure trove of memories. Mike, Cam, and I have our own Rubbermaid bins, filled with the stuff of childhood. Each of the bins includes a baby book, where Mom intended to keep records of our growth and milestones, as well as creepy locks of hair. After the first week, my baby book is empty, and I'm sure my brothers' are as well. I know I was born around 7:00 p.m., but I don't know when I took my first step. And it's only by the grace of the internet that I know the number-one song in the United States on January 12, 1977: "You Make Me Feel Like Dancing" by Leo Sayer.

Each bin also has a School Day Treasures book. I'd like to think my book, like its baby book counterpart, fell victim to the law of diminishing returns. But I acknowledge the possibility that I was such a bad student, there just wasn't anything suitable to put in a book with the word "treasures" in its title.

"Mom," I said recently, "weren't you worried about the fact that I was a terrible student?"

"No," she said. "I knew you'd figure it out."

This feels very old school—trusting me to figure out how to stand on my own two feet. It reminds me of the days when parents trusted their kids to come home at dark and couldn't text them a hundred times to see what they were up to. On one hand, I think Mom could've used a Melita curfew siren for support. On the other hand, I guess I did figure it out eventually.

Every year in elementary school, each kid was given a saddle-stitched yearbook with a soft cover. It was chock-full of photos and had space for classmates to sign their names and include a message. Those yearbooks are in my mom's School Day Treasures book, slipped into the sleeve of each grade. Looking through them, I realize I don't have a single signature from anyone. I don't know why this is, but I can make an educated guess.

Those who know me now might shake their heads in disbelief at this, but I've always been, or at least felt, socially awkward. This is probably related to my anxiety as much as it's related to my childhood identity confusion, a feeling that others wouldn't like me if they really knew me. I didn't try to make friends with kids my own age. That red-headed kid in Melita was burned into my consciousness, along with his slur.

"Burnt toast! Burnt toast!"

My closest childhood friend was my next-door neighbour, Chris Kelly. He's still my friend, and he's still five years younger than me. In kindergarten, each student got a chance to be King (or Queen) for a Day, and show and tell was part of the festivities. Chris, who was just a toddler, was my absolute favourite thing in the entire world, so naturally I brought him to school instead of a toy or a favourite book. That's my earliest memory of Chris: a blond-haired, blue-eyed toddler wearing my King for a Day red cape and gold crown, and me, showing him off to my classmates.

Chris and I were inseparable for years. We snaked our way through the blue play tunnel in his parents' basement. We sat on the couch and watched Winnipeg Jets games or played *Blades of Steel* on the Nintendo console. We climbed the tree in the front yard or used its nooks and crannies as places to hide our action figures. We set up Castle Grayskull on the front steps and pretended that my front yard was Eternia. We placed nets on either side of the Kellys' yard and played soccer. We played *Winter Games* or *California Games* on the Commodore 64. We went psychedelic in Cam's basement bedroom with the strobe light he'd built in shop class.

Chris has told me that half of his childhood memories are of our friendship, and that's a fair estimate for me too. My earliest memory of Chris is King for a Day. The last memory I have of him from my childhood is the day he moved to Sackville, New Brunswick. His family's wood-panelled station wagon pulled away from the curb with all six of the Kelly clan packed inside: Ken, Jo-Ann, Aly, Claire, newborn Meghan, and Chris. He was in the back seat, turned towards me. I was standing on the sidewalk. The rest of my family was on the front step. I took several small steps forward as the station wagon drove off, like I could catch up to it. Chris was staring out the back window in a yellow-and-pink-striped shirt, waving goodbye.

Mom takes a lot of photos. When we were younger, she always had her Nikon camera with her. She may have taken more photographs with that camera than people take with their cellphones today. Stacks of albums in Mom's basement record our lives in moments like works of sequential art. In our family, her most famous photo is one of Mike on the beach, holding a plastic shovel. Another photo of Mike also stands out. He's maybe a year old and is stationed at the kitchen table. There's a tray of watercolour paints in front of him, but only one of those chalky-tasting coloured pucks has been touched: the black one. The paint is all over his face. Earlier in the day, he'd seen a Black man and wanted to look like him.

I think about skin colour and people's reaction to it. Why was Chris, who was so many years younger, not just my best friend but my only friend? There are a number of reasons—the most important being that he was an amazing kid. But he was also safe. I used to think that kids don't see skin colour—they just see another kid. I thought that was something we lost as adults. Part of that's true. Kids do just see another kid, but they also see the colour of that kid's skin. It's just that to a kid, difference is an innocent curiosity. It's a toddler taking out watercolours and trying to look the same as somebody else. Small kids don't wield curiosity in closed fists or sling it in hateful epithets. They don't chase the only Native kid in town all over the pool yelling, "Burnt toast!" They don't, but then they do, sooner or later. It's a learned way of seeing another human being.

THE BINS IN Mom's basement are also full of mementos. Mike's got a lot of old drawings in his. Cam, I'm not sure. He was a skater and an athlete. But he never played video games, didn't draw, didn't write. And I've learned not to look through his stuff anyway. He used to keep, in a safe in his room, the only two graphic novels he ever owned: *Batman: The Cult* and *Batman: The Killing Joke*. The repercussions for even attempting to gain access to those books were severe. My bin has old stories and those elementary school yearbooks, but there isn't a single junior high or high school yearbook. By contrast, my wife, Jill, has all of hers, and they're full of signatures and notes and drawings from friends and classmates.

I've often wondered why that is, why I never bothered to get a yearbook any of those years. Maybe I've wondered too much. The reason could be innocuous; some people just don't care for

them. I texted my friend Kathleen and asked her to send me a
picture of one of our yearbooks for investigative purposes, and
she texted back, "I think I only ever had grade eight, but it'll be
long gone by now."

Everybody has their reasons for keeping a yearbook, for
throwing it away, or for never getting one at all. I suppose one of
the best explanations, on my part, can be found in the yearbook
from my graduation year, which I was eventually able to borrow.
All the graduates' pictures are accompanied by quirky information or song lyrics that reflect both the individual and the time we
were growing up in. My graduation picture has an empty space
beside it. No quirkiness to speak of, no song lyrics. If I could
have a do-over, I'd at least have included a Pearl Jam lyric from
"Black" or "Crazy Mary." What could've been. Absence always
says something, and it can say as much as, or more than, presence.

From a practical standpoint, I wanted the yearbooks so I
could get names right, remember faces, draw out a memory or
two beyond the ones that haven't faded. This was particularly
important for junior high, which was a pivotal time. By then, I
was aware of my indigeneity. That knowledge of being different,
which often created an abject feeling in the pit of my stomach, had
turned specific by then. I knew where my difference came from,
but I did not yet know that I was Cree. Knowing I was Indigenous was enough, and all I wanted to know. I didn't want to
know even that much. Those classmates I was trying to remember
had, as the 1980s stumbled forward into the 1990s, developed a
harmful opinion of Indigenous People. An opinion informed by
everything outside the classroom, and everything within it.

I've been back to River Heights Junior High several times, to
watch my nephew Cameron (Mike's oldest kid) play basketball
or to give a classroom presentation. It's still a big school, with

almost five hundred students. Walking the halls delivered some of those sought-after memories, like the time I was stung by a wasp in the boy's bathroom, threw off my long-sleeved white top, and stood shirtless in a bathroom stall watching my upper arm swell.

One of Jill's closest friends teaches at River Heights now. Amanda was responsible for bringing me to the school to speak, both in 2009, after my first book came out, and most recently in 2018. I texted her and asked if she'd be able to get her hands on the yearbooks from my time there: 1989–90, 1990–91, and 1991–92. A couple of days later, while my daughter Anna was at dance class, I picked the books up from Amanda's house and pored through them, student by student, page by page, grade by grade. I recognized lots of kids—several from that time, but most from Kelvin High School, where I would know them better. I looked for pictures of myself, aside from my class photos, which were required, and found just two in all three yearbooks. One was of me in grade nine, sitting with three other kids at Night Moves Cabaret, an event celebrating our graduation. I'm gangly and smiling at the camera, a cocktail table full of half-eaten pizza in the foreground. Another is the size of a class photo, a filler picture added because there weren't enough kids in the class to take up the last line of the page. It's winter and I'm wearing a Winnipeg Jets hat.

I concentrated my efforts on the eighth grade, which ended in 1991. That's the year I remember most. I was in room 8-14, one of ten grade eight classes. There were about 250 eighth-grade students, and of all those kids, I can recall only three being friends of mine. One of those friends broke my arm in a fight at the outdoor hockey rink on the west side of River Heights Community Centre, away from the prying eyes of school staff. The entire student body was present, encircling us, egging us on to start throwing punches. One guy kept pushing me towards my friend. I kept backing away. Neither of us wanted to throw a punch, so neither of us did. Eventually, I got put into a headlock and thrown to the ground. It was probably the gentlest thing he could've done to me to appease the rabid crowd. *Snap.* That was the second time I broke my arm. Unsurprisingly, these weren't what I'd call close friends, but I guess, at least, they were something. I didn't have any in grade seven.

Wait, that can't be right, I told myself while I flipped through each yearbook, inspecting faces in a desperate attempt to prove myself wrong. Later, while lying in bed after we'd put all the kids to sleep, I voiced my concerns to Jill.

"I really don't think I had any friends in junior high," I said. "Literally the only good friend I can think of pre-high school is Chris."

"Then you probably didn't have any friends," she said.

Jill is pragmatic and brutally honest, and this helps when she's talking me down from a panic attack, but not so much in this case. I suspected she was right, though. Still, I called Mom to confirm. It was late, but I reasoned that she'd still be up listening to the radio or reading. She answered the phone.

"Mom?"

"What is it, David?"

"Did I have any friends in junior high?"

She sighed. "I don't want to talk about this tonight."

"Just name one friend and I'll let you go."

"Have you been bugging Jill too?"

"Yes." Jill had leaned over to talk into the receiver.

"Just one."

She refused again. "Can't we do this another time?"

"That's because I didn't have one!"

"Oh, David."

I had a much easier job recalling times I was picked on or teased or ignored or rejected. My boldest move in junior high was asking out a girl by offering her a box of chocolate-covered cherries (Mom's idea). She was incredibly nice about saying no to me, although her boyfriend was not so pleasant the next day, when he told me, sarcastically, "Hey Robertson, I really liked those chocolates." Nobody likes chocolate-covered cherries. In art class, I popped a girl's cheeks after she'd blown them out like a chipmunk's, because I liked her and boys are stupid and they tease girls when they like them (I still tease Jill, and she doesn't necessarily *love* it). The girl punched me in the face, which I deserved. She would've done well at the rink after school.

I'm not sure I would put any of this on the kids I went to school with. The teasing, getting picked on or intimidated, being ignored. Sure, having my arm broken in a fight didn't help matters. There are cool ways to break your arm (my third and fourth breaks were of the cool variety, I guess, because they happened playing sports), and there are uncool ways to break your arm (getting pushed to the ground in front of hundreds of classmates). I was also chubby from grade six until grade eight. Baby fat, Mom used to tell me. "You'll grow out of it."

I suspect that most of my struggles were a product of social awkwardness from low self-esteem. Who'd want to be friends with, go out with, eat lunch with—do anything with—an Indigenous kid? I can't blame that on everybody I went to school with. I put that on myself. There was some truth to it, though. I heard the racist jokes. I knew what some kids thought about "Indians." I knew because I thought the same thing.

IT WAS WINTER. Far enough from summer that my dark skin had turned a lighter shade of brown. The bell rang to signal the end of class, and students flooded the hallways. There was a metallic chorus of opening and shutting lockers, switching out one textbook in favour of another. I was standing at my own locker outside homeroom, switching binders and textbooks, minding my own business. I felt a tap on my shoulder. A girl from my class was beside me. I was suddenly nervous. My palms began sweating. My pulse shot up. Girls didn't just come up to me and tap me on the shoulder. The last time I'd spoken to a girl was during the disastrous chocolate-covered cherries incident.

"Can I ask you a question?"

"Uhhh, sure."

She stepped closer to me and whispered, "Are you an Indian? Or do you just have a great tan?"

I wonder if in that moment, what Auntie Joan had said echoed in my mind: "People would die to have skin like yours. It's not something you should be ashamed of. You should be proud of it." This girl appreciated the colour of my skin, but that appreciation felt like it had a caveat. One reason was good, the other was bad—and it couldn't be both. I thought about what to say for an uncomfortably long period of time, but in that place, to her, there could really be only one response.

I scoffed. "I'm not an Indian."

Indians didn't go to River Heights Junior High. I didn't know of any others. They all lived on reserves or in the North End. And the North End was something to turn your nose up at. I used to think it was; I know it isn't now.

"Oh," she said. "Cool."

We had a brief conversation about my tan and where I'd got it. I wrote about this exchange in my first novel, *The Evolution of Alice*. I changed my name to Matthew and hers to Tara. In real life, as in the novel, I was relieved when she left. I stood at my locker and replayed the exchange while the hallways emptied and the next class began. But after school, while I walked home, I didn't feel relief. I felt shame. A shame that I'd not felt before.

I was ashamed to be Indigenous. That wouldn't be the last time I'd face questions about my cultural background and do the same damn thing. But there was something more. I was ashamed to have denied self, and back then I couldn't understand why. Not why I'd denied who I was, but why I felt ashamed for having done it. Hadn't I just dodged a bullet?

I'VE REVIEWED THE census data, and it's clear that in the late 1980s, River Heights lacked diversity. Comparatively, it still does. For example, in 2011, Indigenous People—both Métis and First Nations (there were no Inuit people)—made up around 6 percent of the neighbourhood's population, well below the municipal average of 11.1 percent. Visible minorities in the community, not including Indigenous People, made up just over 10 percent. In 1996, Indigenous representation in River Heights was 1 percent. I suppose things are trending upwards, but you can really only go up from one lonely percentage point. The representation in the 1980s was even lower, with just one family identifying as Indigenous. Again: not my family.

If my parents had intended to raise me and my brothers as non-Indigenous, then River Heights was a clever neighbourhood choice. It was a good place to *not* be Indigenous. Living there felt like living in a bubble (I've talked to other people who have lived or currently live in the community, and they agree with this analogy). There were invisible borders that, for the most part, we didn't cross—although stepping over the line in most directions wasn't seen as dangerous. If we went too far west, for example, and crossed Kenaston Boulevard, we'd end up in Tuxedo, an upper-class neighbourhood. Moving up in the world, but unfamiliar. There was even more of a demographic shift to the east, where you crossed Cambridge Street to get to Fort Rouge. But Fort Rouge is still a nice neighbourhood. My auntie Marion, Dad's sister, lives there. And Fort Whyte, south of Taylor Avenue, is every bit as well off as River Heights. Mostly, we were simply comfortable living where we were and preferred not to leave our neighbourhood. But when it came to communities across the Maryland Bridge—the West End, the North End—those were definite no-fly zones. It wasn't just unfamiliarity; to go to these neighbourhoods was to put yourself in peril. If River Heights had an Indigenous population of 1 percent, that felt like 100 percent over the bridge: a big, dirty, poverty-stricken, gang- and drug-infested reserve filled with rundown houses and rundown people.

DURING THE SUMMER between grades eight and nine, I grew several inches and returned to River Heights Junior High lanky and uncoordinated. Mom was right about the baby fat, but other than the physical change, not much was different for me. If anything, both personally and academically, life was getting worse. This was reflected in my grades and the comments teachers made on my report cards. It wasn't a nosedive, but there were more Cs, fewer As. "Disruptive behaviour interferes with the rights of others to learn within a safe environment," wrote my gym teacher, explaining the D he'd given me in the first term. I don't remember being so bad that I created an unsafe environment for my classmates, but I do know that I acted like an idiot. A class clown, not a safety hazard. A kid desperate for attention, desperate to be liked. And it must have somewhat worked, because in grade nine I was invited to a party and that was a first.

Mom dropped me off and planned to pick me up at a prede-termined time: midnight. The gathering took place in a brown townhouse, one in a crowd of several, each dwelling indiscernible from the next. I stood at the front door, my hand clenched into a fist and hovering inches away from the glass, ready but unwilling to knock. I looked back to see Mom pulling away in the Acadian, watched until she was out of sight, and shook the impulse to chase after her. Eventually, I knocked.

The living room was full of kids from school. There were two couches separated by a glass coffee table, and stairs leading to a second floor where nobody was permitted to go. I navigated through the crowd, found one of the couches, sat down closest to the wall, and stayed there. I watched other kids partying for the bulk of the evening, wishing that I could have their confidence. Watched them or checked the time, counting down to when Mom would be back and I could leave and finally take a deep breath.

The minutes passed slowly. I made eye contact with some-body, smiled and quickly looked away. Reached forward and grabbed handfuls of chips from the coffee table. Tried to dis-appear in plain sight. I'm not sure how hard I needed to work to do that. Only one person bothered to speak to me all night: a girl in my grade who was one of those kids who seem to exist only in high school romantic comedies. She was popular, pretty, kind, funny, and incredibly cool, partly because she didn't act like she was too cool for somebody like me. Most likely, she saw how uncomfortable I looked sitting on the couch by myself, staring aimlessly into the crowd, eating chips one by one out of the palm of my hand. It must've been a sad thing to witness. Whatever her intentions—I've no doubt they were good—I took her attention as pity and found little consolation in it.

I learned a new term recently, in talking with a friend of mine, Nicole. I wasn't telling her this story; we were talking about watching somebody embarrass themselves. It very likely involved a YouTube video. It also very likely involved me suggesting that she watch a video I found hilarious. She wasn't having any of it. She called it vicarious embarrassment. It's like that scene in the movie *Swingers*, when Mike leaves more and more painful messages for a girl he's just met at a bar. The scene ends with the girl picking up in the middle of yet another message and telling Mike never to call her again. I get that feeling thinking about those long hours at the party, picturing myself sitting on the couch alone. It's as if there were cellphones back then and somebody took a grainy video of the party and zoomed in on me.

The night wore on. Occasionally, somebody else would arrive and integrate themselves into the party in a way that I never could. At one point, a First Nations kid showed up. His name was Vince, and he walked into the room looking confident and tough, his baseball cap turned backwards, baggy pants, a jersey of some kind tucked underneath a black jacket. Wherever that townhouse was, it wasn't that far outside of River Heights. That meant Vince was a long way from home. He almost certainly had come from the North End. And yet, I'd seen him around River Heights before, I was sure of it. The context is lost on me, but those sightings, coupled with the expectations I had placed on him based on my own ignorance, made me terrified of his presence. This is not an overstatement.

Initially, I avoided eye contact with him while simultaneously keeping track of where he was in the room in case he got too close. And then what? What was he going to do? My heart was racing, my limbs were shaking, my palms were sweating. Mom wasn't coming for a while yet. If time had been moving slowly before, it was frozen now.

I decided I had to get off the couch and actually hide somewhere not in plain sight. I timed my move for when Vince was across the room, when he and I were separated by a throng of teenagers. I stood up, walked out of the living room, climbed a few steps up the stairs, and sat down. There was a half wall between the stairs and the living room, a partition that concealed me from the party. At some point, the rom-com girl, walking from the living room to the kitchen, saw me.

"What are you doing over here?"

In retrospect, it was a really bad hiding place. I didn't want to answer her. I didn't want her to know why I was sitting on the stairs. Nothing good could come from it if I admitted that I was afraid of some kid I didn't know. Time wasn't really frozen. Mom would eventually pull up in front of the townhouse in the Acadian and whisk me away to safety.

"Come on," she said. "Tell me."

I caved. I didn't even hold out that long.

"I'm afraid of that Vince guy," I admitted. "If he sees me, he's going to beat me up."

She gave me an "are you kidding me?" kind of look. Then she was gone, and I was alone again. I hadn't been chastising myself for long when Vince himself appeared, climbed the stairs, and sat down beside me.

"You're scared of me?"

I glanced at him, then away from him. I nodded slightly.

He didn't ask me why I was scared of him. As I've become more involved in the Indigenous community, been followed around a store in my own neighbourhood, been called a "fucking monkey" at one of my first book signings by a stranger who had no interest in buying my book—in short, as I've encountered some of what Vince had probably dealt with his whole life—I've learned why he didn't need to ask. But he didn't look angry. Just resigned.

"You don't have to be," he said.

"I know."

I didn't know.

Vince stood up and walked to the bottom of the stairs. It looked like he was going to leave me like that, head back into the masses filled with beer and chips, into the blaring music. It looked like he was going to leave me to sit and wait for Mom's Acadian to show up. But he stopped.

"You coming, or are you going to keep hiding up there?"

I may not have said another word to him that night, nor he to me, but I didn't stay on the stairs either. And maybe it's okay to admit that all I did was return to the couch. It's not like that five minutes with Vince made me suddenly confident and social. But something else kept me withdrawn that night, and I couldn't put my finger on it.

When Mom came to get me, I was as quiet in the passenger seat as I had been at the party.

"How'd it go?" she asked, knowing how nervous I'd felt beforehand.

I'm not sure if I answered her. I probably did. I don't keep much from Mom. What I know for certain is that while she looked for an answer from me, I wanted my own answers, and to a different question.

When I was little, Mom used to read me the book *My Mama Says There Aren't Any Zombies, Ghosts, Vampires, Creatures, Demons, Monsters, Fiends, Goblins, or Things*. Maybe the longest title ever for a children's book. Certainly the scariest children's book. (She also read me Maurice Sendak's *Outside Over There*, so she clearly preferred messed-up children's books.) At any rate, in *My Mama Says*, there is one particular being that was the most terrifying to me: the fiend. It had bushy eyebrows, a crocodile-like snout with razor-sharp teeth, high heels, absurdly long fingers, and a fedora with its own scary face. Fiends haunted me while asleep and while awake, and I was certain they lived in Grandma and Grandpa Eyers's basement. One day, Grandma wanted me to grab something from the deep freeze. Popsicles, I think. Unfortunately, the deep freeze was in the darkest corner of the storage room—the worst place possible for a kid afraid of fiends. For the longest, most unreasonable period of time, I stood at the top of the stairs, looking down into the basement. I stayed there until Grandma finally saw me and asked what I was doing.

"Grandma, if I go down there, a fiend is going to get me."

I could picture the scene in the book. The fiend appearing from a closet, dancing towards the kid's bed. The kid pulling the covers right up to his nose, peeking out with one eye at the monster. Even the teddy bear looked like it was about to piss itself.

"There's no such thing as fiends," she said matter-of-factly.

Untrue. I'd read about them. I'd seen pictures of them. They gave me a palpable sense of dread. Grandma may as well have told me that there was no such thing as fear.

"Yes, there is," I said.

"If you go down there, you'll see there's nothing in the basement."

I was always going to lose the argument. I took the stairs step by step, excruciatingly slowly, in true horror-movie fashion. When my foot hit carpet at the bottom of the stairs, my slow descent turned into a fast walk past the piano, into the storage room, by Grandpa's work bench (where he carved shoes and ducks), and up to the deep freeze. I frantically dug through the frozen foods until I found the Popsicles, then I ran back through the basement and up the stairs. No fiend killed me. I didn't even see one. What I had expected was not what I had experienced.

When I saw Vince at that party, I was certain, beyond a shadow of a doubt, that he was going to beat the living shit out of me for one reason alone: he was an Indian. I'd read about them. I'd seen them on the news. My friends and I had talked about them. I knew all about them. Then I spent a few minutes with a kid about my age on the stairs of a party, and everything changed.

I KNEW THAT Dad and I were Indians, but neither of us fit into my narrow view of what an Indian was, so I was able to dissociate from my identity with relative ease. Or run from it. I lived in River Heights, not the North End. Yeah, I lived in a single-parent household for most of my childhood and saw Dad only on the weekends, but even still, he was a professional. I didn't know what he did for a living, but I'd seen him wear a suit for work. He always looked put together, not like those drunken people I'd seen downtown. In fact, I never once saw Dad have a drink. So he was an Indian, sure, but was he really?

I have enough memories of Dad to know that he didn't fit into the stereotypes I'd learned, but there will never be enough of just having him around. I have the memory of him pulling away from the curb with Mike and Cam in the car and me watching them leave. I can see us stalking the fairways at Cottonwood Golf Course, me with Dad's old set of Wilson clubs. We used to stop at Robin's Donuts on the way out of the city. But that's pretty much it. That's all I'll ever have. And it's frustrating because I know he was around more.

I played sports. Soccer. Hockey. In ninth grade, I made the A-team as a goalie. Dad loves watching sports. As a grandfather, he's at the soccer field watching my niece Emma or my nephew Elijah. He's at the rink watching Cole or my nephew Owen. He's in the stands watching my nephew Cameron play basketball. He's at the pool watching my daughter Emily play water polo. He's at the Centennial Concert Hall watching Anna dance. I know Dad watched me play hockey and soccer when I was younger. But I can't picture him.

Maybe that has more to do with me than him. In grade eight, I scored a hat trick. I still remember the third goal. I rush in from the blue line, deke out a defender, fake a forehand shot, go backhand, and slip the puck across the goal line. I turn to the stands while taking off my right glove and tucking it under my left armpit. Cam is on his feet, clapping his hands, smiling. Proud. I raise my arm and extend three fingers, one for each goal. Is my dad there?

Chris told me he could picture us watching Olympic figure skating. He and I were on the floor in my living room, in front of the television. Dad was on the couch, providing background commentary. Shayne remembered seeing Dad when he and Auntie Joan would drive into Winnipeg from Melita. One time, Shayne told me, all four of us boys attacked Dad in Mom's bedroom, and he let one rip. We ran out yelling, "The squid has inked!"

Shayne knew that my brothers and I were First Nations. Once when he and Cam were in a fight, Cam made fun of Shayne's weight, and Shayne made a rude gesture in reply. I can picture what that gesture would have been; I'm sure you can as well. Flatten your hand, fan it over your mouth, and make a war cry. You know, like Indians do in movies. Shayne regrets it, but he also told me, as we reflected on why he would have done it, that it was indicative of the time we were living in. (If you want a refresher, watch "What Makes the Red Man Red?," a classic *Peter Pan* song, on YouTube.) "You've got to remember," he said, "that when we were growing up, people were still singing, 'One little, two little, three little . . .'" Then he stopped and left me to fill in the blanks, and I did. I can. I saw the same movies, sang the same songs. I remember doing a rain dance on the sidewalk out front of our bungalow in River Heights and making the same gesture that Shayne had made to Cam. I had no clue what an actual rain dance was, how it was done by Indigenous People, its origins or meaning.

While I can fill in the blanks to a racist song from a Disney movie or feel the rain splash underfoot while dancing through a puddle, I am left with almost nothing when it comes to memories of Dad from my formative years. I would never begrudge Chris or Shayne for their memories of him, but they feel like stolen recollections that I should have. I want an everyday moment burned into my mind—a banal moment that seems to mean nothing, but means everything. I want to make something up, pretend it's real, just so I can hold on to something other than absence and what it left me with. I picture myself walking into the basement to find Dad napping in front of the television. It's turned to *NCIS: Los Angeles*. I lean over and startle him awake with a kiss on his cheek. He swats me away and mumbles, half-asleep, "What're you doing?" But that's not from my childhood. That's from last year. I can't bring myself to make something up.

I'm able to articulate now what was going through my head back in grade nine, as I left that party in Mom's Pontiac Acadian. Something was missing, and while I might have been aware of it, I hadn't recognized until that moment how much it had affected me. It was missing when I asked Auntie Joan why my skin was so ugly. It was missing when I told the girl by my locker that I wasn't an Indian. But its absence had never been more apparent than when I made a connection between how I'd judged Vince and how the red-headed kid at the Melita pool had treated me.

Were that kid's attitude and mine all that different? Did those attitudes come from a different place, in a different way, when you strip it all down? Something had been learned from a source—maybe a song in *Peter Pan*, maybe a *Firestorm* comic book, maybe a story on the six o'clock news—and whatever had been learned was passed down to someone else. And so a red-headed kid with sunburnt skin chased a brown-skinned kid around a pool in a small town in southwest Manitoba. And years later, that same brown-skinned kid hid on a stairway in a town-house somewhere outside of his safe little bubble, simply because another kid looked a certain way.

On the way home from the party, from my encounter with Vince, on our way back to the safety of River Heights, I sat silent. My forehead was pressed against the cool surface of the passenger window, and I was staring at the houses as they approached and then receded. I kept replaying the moment Vince walked up the stairs towards me in my pathetic little hiding place. I kept thinking about the terror I'd felt before he asked me if I was afraid of him. Yes, I told him. Yes, I was afraid of him. But then I wasn't. No, I told her. No, I'm not an Indian. But I was. There was a connection between the two. There was something that connected everything, but I didn't know what it was. Just that it was missing.

"Mom?" I said as we drew closer to home.

"Yes?" she said.

"I want to talk to Dad."

I WAITED FOR him on the couch in the basement. I heard the doorbell ring, then the front door open. Mom and Dad greeted each other in muffled voices as he walked inside. Their footsteps trailed from the entryway through the living room above my head, across the kitchen, and finally down the stairs. My heart began to race. My fingers were trembling. There was a heaviness in the air. I could feel it. Dad could too. It dictated our greeting, sombre and delicate. He sat beside me on the couch, shifted his body towards me. Mom sat on the other couch to give us space.

"Mom said you had something you wanted to talk to me about," he prompted.

I nodded. I was staring down at my hands, clasped together, holding tight to the moment so it wouldn't slip away. He put his hand on my hands. I started to sob. I spoke through tears and a heaving chest.

"I don't think you've been a good father to me."

"I know. I'm sorry."

I don't know what it felt like for him to hear that. As a father myself, I can only guess. Even today, I won't ask him. He wasn't there enough. I know how much he regrets that. I know he regrets it as much as I regret the time I missed with him. The memories I won't ever have. There was so much I didn't know. Not only about where he'd been and why he and Mom weren't together, but also about him. About him, and because of that, about me.

NĒWO (FOUR)

I forgot to arrange a ride from the airport to the York Boat
Inn. Dad looks unfazed, as if he knows something I don't.
I try to match his demeanour, standing in the middle of the
airport lobby, surrounded by its minimalist decor: a smattering
of white and green chairs and benches, a coffeemaker atop a
microwave stand, and white walls as mind-numbing as the flu-
orescent lighting. To break the monotony, there are two maps
affixed to them with push-pins—one of reserves in Manitoba
listed by their First Nations names, another of Canada as a
whole. Dad's right not to worry. While I'm just about to email
my cousin Darlene for a ride into town, a non-Indigenous man
asks us if we need a lift.

Kyle drives a white Manitoba government truck, a vehicle not
uncommon in the community; there seem to be as many trucks

as there are trees. Dad and I put our luggage into the cargo bed and pile into the front seat, Dad in the middle and me on the passenger side. Kyle, a short, stocky man with five o'clock shadow, has a friendly way about him. The moment we pull away from the airport, he and Dad start talking about how he came to live in Norway House; it turns out he married into the community after working here with Manitoba Infrastructure. Dad explains that he grew up here in the 1930s, 1940s, and early 1950s, but never came back to live on the reserve after that. Some things have changed since that time, he says, but many things have stayed the same. I get the sense that Dad's content, maybe even relieved, that Norway House has clung to the past. I feel like it's clung to him too.

We slow down to pass Robertson Bay, where Dad and the family lived when they weren't on the trapline, and where they moved permanently after 1944. I've asked Dad more than once if Robertson Bay was named after our family, but I know it's coincidental. The entrance to the bay is almost hidden, disappearing into the thick trees. A dog stands at attention on the gravel road. I look back at the entrance as we drive ahead, and I think of the stories Dad has shared with me.

I can picture him as a child, swimming along the shores of the bay, jumping from rock to rock with his siblings. I've been down to those shores with him. I've watched him look out over the water. I've seen his face. It makes me feel a part of those memories, as if they're as much mine as they are his. And maybe there's some truth to that.

Isn't that what blood memory is? The experiences of one generation felt by the next, and the next after that. Experiences, teachings, woven into the fabric of our DNA, ingrained in us through the stories we pass down as gifts. We tell the same stories, but they change over time, depending on the person, depending on the context. They change over time but become no less significant. There is truth to that.

I WAS WITH Dad and Mom in the living room of the house I grew up in on Queenston Street. Dad had just finished grumbling, "I don't like this—I don't want any attention," and he got up from the kitchen table, where we'd eaten lunch together and spent an hour on the subject of his childhood and Norway House.

Then—with Dad in a cushioned chair, Mom on the love seat, me getting my coat on by the dining room table—Dad said, in the middle of a short and rare silence, "I have memories of my childhood, but it's hard to place them."

"Yeah," I said, trying to act like this wasn't a big moment, even though it felt like it was. He was offering unsolicited information to me. I finished putting on my coat, slipped it over my shoulders. "It's the same for me. I've got these images that I know happened, but I just don't know when or where. I think memories work that way."

"I'm sitting on a hill," Dad said, "looking out over the water. I'm waiting for something, but I don't know what."

I sat down at the table and pulled out a piece of paper that Dad had used to draw a map earlier. I flipped it over, took a pen out of my pocket, and wrote down verbatim what he had just said. Luckily, I was able to read it later. (I write everything on a laptop, and my penmanship is barely legible.)

Dad could picture himself as a child on a hill and knew he was looking out over the water, knew he was waiting for something, but he couldn't remember what that something was. Whatever he was waiting for had surely had an impact on him all those years ago. It made me think of my first memory. I was running down the hallway towards the living room, towards Mom, but I can't remember what I was running from. We are formed by the events of the past and how we remember them in the present, or what we can remember. What we don't know can influence us as much as what we do know.

When Dad and I discuss reconciliation, he talks about it, within the context of healing, as an act of remembering. We learn more about today when we know about yesterday. We know more about the direction we are headed if we understand where we are now. Yesterday has led us to today, and today will lead us to tomorrow. I believe this is true on an individual, family, and community level. I address the subject of identity within this same framework. Who you are, your identity, is informed by your own experiences and the experiences of those who came before you were born. If you want to understand yourself, take the initiative to seek out what came before you. How does that inform your identity, the decisions you have made and will continue to make?

In telling the story of Dad's life and how it's entwined with my own, I've come to the realization that it's necessary to talk about what came before him. Understanding that—finding out as much as I can—will help me better understand him, and ultimately myself. Some of that information is available through records I've been able to uncover, through research I've conducted, and appropriately, through stories I've been told that have been passed down from one generation to the next. This is the way we used to learn from one another in the Cree culture and the many other Indigenous cultures across Turtle Island. But some of what I want to know, what I feel I need to know, is not so easily discovered. Memory is a tricky thing. Records were lost or never kept at all. Some of what I have come to know, I have come to know through more intangible means. You might call it a series of educated guesses, and that would be a fair description. But I think it's something more.

For starters, Nana barely talked about her time at Norway House Indian Residential School to anybody. Ever. All I have is one picture of her, in 1932, on the day of her graduation. All traces of that time in her life—records of her experiences while attending residential school—were lost in a fire and upon her death. But in researching the school itself, I came to some conclusions about what her time there might have looked like. Although it would be fair to call these educated guesses, I believe these conclusions are closer to the feeling of homecoming I had when I first set foot in Norway House. Blood memory. When I stand in the place where the residential school used to be, I'm sure that I can feel Nana there, walking the halls, sleeping in the dorm, attending classes.

Dad was born on May 18, 1935, but his story, and mine, began long before that. Several initial obstacles announced themselves while I was researching his mother, Sarah Robertson, née Captain, and her life prior to 1935. Documentation was poor for First Nations people living in communities, in particular outside of the residential school system. Researchers have to rely on documentation archived by non-Indigenous sources—the Hudson's Bay Company and the United Church, for example. In Norway House Cree Nation, the difficulties are compounded because although the federal government kept a mountain of records relating to the residential school system, the Norway House school burned down. Twice. And its records burned with it. As a result, mentions of Sarah Captain are sparse; the most significant record I discovered—the photograph of her in 1932—came from the United Church Archives.

History has been lost. It died in those fires, or died with family members who passed away without sharing their truths. Nana died on June 15, 1985, and in her death, the story of her experience at Norway House Indian Residential School, and possibly at Towers Island Day School before it, will remain untold. The only person with whom Nana shared anything significant about her time in school was my mother. I'll address what Mom was told, but suffice to say it was very little.

I know why. Just as residential school history was ignored in educational systems across Canada, it was a history that survivors didn't talk about. From what I understand, from what I've read and what I've heard from survivors, trauma in all its forms was associated with those experiences. In the 1980s, we didn't know, as we do now, the power in sharing those truths, the healing that sharing those truths can bring. Whatever Nana went through, she kept her experiences to herself for over fifty years, and they were buried with her.

SARAH CAPTAIN WAS born on July 11, 1914, to Frederick and Flora Captain in Gods Lake Narrows, a First Nations community northwest of Norway House and at the southeast corner of Gods Lake. By 1921, the Captain family—Frederick (34), Flora (21, but she would die one year later), Sarah (7), Maggie (5), and Henry George (1)—had moved to Norway House Cree Nation. As status Indians, Sarah and her siblings would have been legally required to attend residential school.[1] This is true of most First Nations

---

[1] For survivors and their families, the next section may be triggering. A Residential School Crisis Line has been set up to support former students and their family members. If you need help, call 1-866-925-4419.

children pre-1950. There doesn't appear to have been a residential school in the small community of Gods Lake Narrows, only a day school. As a result, Sarah was forced to attend the closest one: Norway House Indian Residential School.

In 1913, the school was in a state of disrepair, and officials intended to rebuild it. The building was so poorly insulated that during the winter, thirteen wood-burning stoves were in use at any given time, and because of this there was a serious risk of fire. The situation was so dire, according to one report, that if a fire started, the school would go up in flames in *mere minutes*. At the time, the dormitory windows were barred, presumably to keep children from running away, and there was serious concern that if a fire broke out, the children could not be saved. Unsurprisingly, and as feared, the school burned to the ground that same year. Miraculously, it appears that no students died. Two years later, a newly built residential school opened, along with an adjoining day school.

Risk of fire gave way to different problems. In the new school's first year of operation, 1916, enrolment was one hundred students even though the capacity was eighty. Some children were sleeping two to a bed. Over-enrolment continued even when one community held back its children. They had complained of being fed rotten fish, and many of them showed signs of frostbite. Reverend Lousley, principal of Norway House Indian Residential School, sent a letter to Jacob Berens, Chief of Berens River, that read: "You have long hindered the children of your people from attending these great schools that God has provided . . . So I, one of the men God has sent to your people in this North Land, call you to repent of this your wrongdoing before it is too late." Chief Berens replied: "I am glad I will eventually be judged by a higher judge than yourself."

Inevitably, overcrowding led to health issues, and clothing and food (rotten or fresh) became scarce. No matter. Successors to Reverend Lousley continued to increase enrolment to as many as 110 students. Their rationale was suspect. In one case, James Blackford, principal of the school from 1925 to 1930, argued that there were more beds for girls, and they should be able to enrol more as a result. However, girls were sleeping out on the balcony even during the winter months.

The day school absorbed students who couldn't fit into the residential school's two classrooms, although it's unclear if this too was used to make the case for more students. But it might explain why Sarah's siblings, Maggie and Henry George, attended a day school that wasn't attached to the residential school. Rather, records show they attended Towers Island Day School, a one-room schoolhouse located on the southern tip of Towers Island, at the mouth of Jack River and the southernmost end of the reserve.

Information about this particular day school, and frankly all the day schools that operated in Norway House, is severely limited. It's a minor miracle that I located a record of Henry George and Maggie's enrolment at Towers Island at all. The only other document I've found that mentions Towers Island is the *Handbook for Prospective Teachers in Indian Schools*, a sort of long-form recruitment brochure urging teachers to participate in what many documents call "Indian work." It paints a bleak picture of life in Norway House:

> *Towers Island School consists of one classroom with attached teacherage. It is heated by a large heater situated at the back of the room as there is no basement. Grades 1–8 are taught here. Water from the river is used for drinking and washing*

*purposes. There is no plumbing for the building. The teacher-
age has one small kitchen, a living room and a small bedroom
with part of the latter used as a clothes closet. It is heated with
an oil burner and a kitchen cook stove. There is no basement
in the teacherage and therefore storage space is limited.*

In 1931, one year before Nana graduated, administrators
started giving serious consideration to student health at Norway House Indian Residential School. The school was put on a
half-day system, but the concerns remained. A report written by
Indian agent William Gordon in 1933 outlined how the school
fell short educationally, morally, physically, and economically. As
such, Gordon concluded, the school could not fulfill its main
function of "advancing the Indian."

This report is an odd but telling mix of the realities of
the school's conditions and the ignorance of the writer. For
example, Gordon believed the school was detrimental to the
students' moral development because the segregation of boys
and girls advanced the "sex idea." That is to say, the students
were apart for so long that when they came together, sex was
all that was on their minds. Religious training wasn't working.
The girls who attended the school were cleaner than those who
didn't, and so more attractive to the boys, who had no desire
to be moral.

Gordon then pointed to another shortcoming, one not
moral in nature but physical. From a health standpoint, students
should have been "superior to those children brought up on
the reserves." They slept better and lived in a cleaner environment than the "small and practically sealed rooms" where children were growing up on reserve. But stating that they should
have been "superior" strongly implies that they were not. Why

weren't they? Gordon projects a sense of bewilderment throughout his report, and if I were him, I would have been confused
too. What he failed to recognize, however, as he extolled the
benefits of the residential school, were the advantages that kids
living on reserve, out on the trapline, enjoyed. The education
and quality of life they received through living in a traditional
way. Ironically, Gordon recommended that students be encouraged to work and play more outdoors—an unusual conclusion
given the government's thoughts on "advancing the Indian" at
school. Weren't kids growing up on reserve the ones who were
already outdoors? Weren't they supposedly starving? Living in
unsanitary conditions?

In 1934, Gordon pitched an experimental program that, if
all went well, would eventually be replicated in Norway House
Indian Residential School. It amounted to land-based education—something that today we know is of enormous benefit
to Indigenous students. The plan was to start in Island Lake, a
community with 240 kids, most of whom attended day schools.
The reasoning was that Island Lake people were "primitive but
teachable." Under this plan, a few pupils would be taught car-
pentry, masonry, furniture making, skiff and boat building, cul-
tivation of land, care of gardens and later of grains, fishing, care
of nets, trapping, care of furs and skins, and later, care of various
animals. Nowhere did the plan mention involving Elders, even
though they and their ancestors had been doing much of this
work for thousands of years. No, the kids needed to be taught by
white educators.

But all these issues paled in comparison with the biggest
threat to the children's welfare: students at the school were being
abused. In the winter of 1906, Charles Clyne ran away from the

school after a staff member punished him for wetting his bed and allegedly stealing clothing. Charles may have committed the great sin of being cold, given the condition the old school was in before it burned down. He spent the night hiding in a cabin, in the bush, in the middle of winter. His feet froze, and he became permanently disabled. During the investigation that followed, John Semmens, inspector of Indian Agencies, got Reverend Lousley to admit to thrashing the boy many times, but Lousley contended that Charles "deserved all he received as he was the very worst pupil in the school." Semmens argued that the student should have been given early dismissal if he was that undesirable, that he should have received medical attention for his bed-wetting, and that the school should have made more of an effort to find him after he'd gone missing. Reverend Lousley might have done better using more "Christian" methods.

Lousley was once more the subject of scrutiny when, after the new school opened, he had a boy tied up to prevent him from running away. This act was defended by an official with the Methodist Missionary Society, who explained, "This was the only time that this was done, and it was during a time that the ice was rotten in the bay and they were afraid that his foolishness might lead him to run away over the ice, and thus lose his life." I suppose they didn't want another child to freeze his feet to the point of disability.

In 1930, long after Lousley was gone, a male student claimed that the principal had struck him in the head with his fist, knocked him down, and then dragged him to another room. In that room, the student was further beaten with a strap. This egregious physical violation was witnessed by other students, who testified to it in court. But the charges were subsequently dismissed, with the judge warning the alleged abuser to refrain from beating students with his fist. That's what straps are for.

It's unlikely that Nana went through her time at Norway House Indian Residential School without encountering some form of abuse. Maybe she was one of the girls sleeping on the balcony in winter or sharing a single bed with a classmate. There's a possibility that she didn't eat well, given that the school was always at least 25 percent over capacity. Or perhaps Nana made it through school without experiencing the trauma that many students did. That seems unlikely, but we'll never know.

What we do know is that if the victim wasn't Nana, it was another child, and if it was any one child, it was one child too many. It feels inappropriate to assume the trauma of one, even if that one is my grandmother, when the trauma of others is a certainty. I wish I'd had the chance to talk to her about her life and her time at the school. I wish she'd shared more with the one person she did talk to about her experiences. But she didn't.

What Nana did share with my mother was mostly about her little sister, Maggie. As it turns out, several family members were unaware that Sarah had even had a sister. Just a brother. Henry George lived a long life. Born June 19, 1920, he passed away on August 28, 2010. I went to visit him on my most recent trip to Norway House, in December 2018. It took a bit of searching, but I found his grave at the North Cemetery, the newest cemetery, surrounded by a white picket fence, as are many graves in the community. But despite searching every cemetery in Norway House for Maggie's grave, including the old cemetery in Rossville, I could not find it. It is likely unmarked.

"What did Nana tell you about her time at residential school?" I asked Mom.

"Oh, not much," Mom said. "Just that she was looking for her sister, and that she couldn't find her."

According to Nana, Maggie died while attending Towers Island Day School. Her name is listed in the 1921 and 1926 census data, but then she disappears. In 1926, she would have been nine or ten years old. If Sarah graduated in 1932 and was looking for Maggie while still in school, that means Maggie died sometime between 1926 and 1932. Recently, I requested her death certificate from Manitoba Vital Statistics. On the report I got back, her date of birth is listed as 1916 (no month or day given), and her date of death is unknown. The report states that Maggie's age at death was between seven and twelve (meaning she died between 1923 and 1928). She never lived to be a teenager. Mom and Dad don't know how Maggie died. Sarah didn't either. She was looking for her sister. She didn't find out until years later that her sister had passed away. It is the one pain I am certain Nana experienced as a child. It is the one fact I've been left with, without question.

During that same trip to Norway House in December 2018, I parked my car beside Jack River, received assurances from a community member that I wouldn't fall through the ice, and walked across the frozen water to Towers Island. When I reached land, I climbed an embankment and saw the remains of Towers Island Day School through thick snow that seemed to be falling in slow motion. Only the stone foundation was left. Sections of it were covered with snow and undergrowth, but so much of it was still visible, the cracked, cold concrete like a maze with no end and no beginning. I walked to the middle of the site, stood on the concrete, and turned around in a full circle. Somewhere through the bush there was a church that people from the community still attended. Kids from the day school once attended that same church. I imagined them walking from the school, through the bush, in a straight line. A cold, hard line like the concrete foundation on which I stood. I tried to picture what the school would have looked like. I tried to build up walls from the stone foundation. I tried to picture Maggie there. I'd spent over an hour at the old cemetery looking for her, stopping at each child's unmarked grave and wondering if it was hers. Chances are that I was close to her during that time. But the truth is, standing in the middle of the ruins, at the southern tip of Towers Island, was the closest I would ever feel to her. I could picture Nana walking through the rooms, looking for her sister, trying to find her way through the maze but failing. There was nobody to find. Maggie was already gone.

I HAVEN'T BEEN fair. There was more to Nana than her time at government-run schools in Norway House Cree Nation. Dad has told me more than once that our story, his and mine, our family's, isn't a residential school story. He's right—it isn't. That history is a part of our family, and it always will be. But there is more to it, more to us, and there was more to Nana. I've talked to several family members about her—Mom, Dad, Auntie Effie and Auntie Marion, Uncle Robert, my cousins. To a person, they described Nana in the same way. Kind. Gentle. Loving. Generous. Wonderful with children. "All I remember is her rocking in her rocking chair and braiding my hair."

She never got after her children. Never raised her voice to them. Always wore a dress, never pants, except once on Halloween for a costume. If you were interested in something, she would teach you. Her children and grandchildren learned knitting from her, and sewing. How to make a doll. She might've regretted that last lesson. One day, Auntie Effie was playing with a doll she'd made, warming it by the fire, pretending it was cold. Within minutes, the house had burned down and the whole family was homeless. They had to move back into the older, smaller house on Robertson Bay.

Above all else, Nana wanted her children and grandchildren to get educated. She understood the necessity of education and the difficulties of being First Nations in the new world they faced. To the Olsen girls, my cousins, she once said, "It's really nice that you want to learn about your Indian side, but don't let it get in the way of your education."

I've heard all this from her family, but I've heard it straight from her as well. Months before she died, she made a tape that she then distributed to all of her children. In it, she talks about the importance of being with family, of being friends with everybody. "Children, remember," she says, "remember to be nice to your parents and your Elders. That's the most important thing in life. Not only your parents and your Elders, but everyone you meet. At school or on the street or wherever it may be." She talks about happiness in place of loneliness. About dreaming of Christmas, when she would see her entire family. She talks about education. "Children, my grandchildren, remember to study. Your education is important. That is the only way you'll make your life worthwhile—if you finish your education, take your grade twelve and on," she says. "Learn. Please learn."

The tape feels at once like a love letter to her family and a final call to action for it. Her voice is powerful and frail. Passionate and tired. She chose happiness and joy over the pain she must have experienced through loss. Her sister, Maggie. Several of her children: Frederick (who was just a baby), Effie Maria, Cameron. She lost her husband, James, when they were still relatively young. But she lived to see several of her children, including Dad, find success through the education she insisted they get. This brought her a deep sense of pride.

I've listened to the tape she made a number of times. It's of terrible quality. In places, you can hardly hear her. But you can hear enough to know what mattered most to her. Family. Kindness. Happiness. Education. Faith. At one point, Nana talks about the importance of asking for help when you need it. From parents, Elders, and God. This should come as no surprise because Norway House was one of the first Christianized reserves in Canada. Perhaps fittingly, then, Nana sounds most alive at the end of the recording, when she says, "Now, I'm going to sing my favourite hymn. This is it . . ." And she sings "Amazing Grace."

Each time I listen to her sing, I think of what I've learned, what she might have experienced, and what I know she did. There were difficulties at the school, and many students struggled as a result, but still, she took grade eight twice to stay there longer. Did her desire for education—a desire she would have for her children and her children's children—help her to find the good within the bad? Happiness in place of loneliness? Or was she lucky enough to avoid what other students could not? I listen to her sing; I listen to the words. I repeat the words in time with Nana, as though there is more to uncover in them. About her. About Dad. About me. But in those words, I find the same confusion, the same questions that I'll probably always have. "T'was grace that taught my heart to fear, and grace, my fears relieved." It would seem that the school took something but gave something back. Each time I listen to her sing, no matter how much I want her to say more, say something to me, say anything else, the song ends. So does the tape.

"Thank you," she says. "That's all for now."

NIYANAN (FIVE)

The remainder of the short drive feels impersonal compared to passing by Robertson Bay, but it's no less interesting. Dad points out one thing after another and discusses them with me and Kyle. The Hudson's Bay Company fort, locally referred to as the Fort, near the banks of the Nelson River. The company's principal inland depot for the fur trade, it's now a historical site populated by three buildings: the Archway Warehouse, the Gaol, and the Powder Magazine. They're all old, dark, and musky abandoned structures under hipped roofs. Rubble-stone masonry with thick granite walls. One of the buildings, the Gaol, has the year 1855 chiselled over the doorway and iron bars on narrow windows.

There was an election recently, and candidate signs still speckle the roadside, left stubbornly erect although months outdated.

They cluster together at high-traffic areas in bouquets of corrugated plastic and wood. We encounter one such assortment as we take a left onto the main road into Rossville, heading into the final leg of our short journey. There are as many community members walking along the roadside in both directions as there are election signs.

People on the move are typically either coming from or going to the mall across the street from the York Boat Inn; its main attractions are the Northern Store, the bank, and a relatively new Tim Hortons. My auntie Flora frequents the coffee shop. Not much younger than Dad, she begins her daily trip to the mall on foot but is always picked up before long. Back in February, I tried to find Auntie one day by driving to the mall and back, hoping to spot her having a coffee or walking. I eventually caught up with her at home. She had just returned with her bingo cards, eager to play with most of the community as the numbers were called over the local radio station, CJNC-FM, 97.9 on the dial.

Now we pull up to the York Boat Inn, stop under the carport in front of the doors, and get our luggage out of the cargo bed. The hotel sits at the far corner of a large parking lot shared with the community's multiplex, which houses the radio station, the ice rink, and a restaurant. As recently as February and as far back as 2000, the restaurant was a Salisbury House, a Manitoba institution, run by an older Chinese man, but it has been rebranded as the York Boat Diner. So much else about the community appears unchanged—the parking lot, multiplex, and hotel all look the same to me as they did eighteen years ago—yet Norway House's new Chief is making his mark. I notice construction happening in earnest adjacent to the restaurant.

"What's going on there?" I ask Kyle, pointing to the gaping hole in the ground where the parking lot ends.

"They're building a community hall," he explains. He says it will host social functions and celebrations like weddings, bingo nights, graduations, dances.

We thank him. He went out of his way to bring us here and never acted as though it was an imposition, welcomed the company and the task of bringing us here. He drives away, leaving me and Dad standing under the carport, luggage at our feet.

Dad goes inside the hotel to check in, undoubtedly eager to have some alone time, to disappear into the quiet for a while. I stay outside, my hand clasped around the extended suitcase handle. There have been times when I've needed it as a crutch while travelling, when anxiety hits me on my way to or while inside an airport. I was glad to have had it as I walked from the overflow parking towards Perimeter Airlines earlier today. But I don't need it for that right now. I'm just holding on to it while I scan the area known as Rossville. The far end of the multiplex, where the radio station is, where in February I talked to the host about how I'd spend the next two days working with kids at the Helen Betty Osborne Ininiw Education Resource Centre and Jack River School; the prefab houses, just far enough from each other to have room to breathe; the community buildings, like the women's shelter and the daycare; the old cemetery, where many of the graves are marked by nameless wooden crosses or cracked and tilted headstones grown over by dead grass; and the church overlooking Little Playgreen Lake, as though admiring its beauty.

After taking all this in, I look up. A clear day has welcomed us to the community, the setting sun has blanketed Norway House with an autumn-coloured sky, and before I turn to go inside the hotel, I think that there is in fact beauty all around.

"YOU COULD PICTURE the scene in your mind. The quiet cove, the tents, the huts with smoke lazing up in the blue sky. The faint smell of pines on the soft wind. As kids, we learned from the Elders the things we needed to know. We learned by doing and by listening and by watching. We learned in the quiet, by the lake, listening to the wind, at our home."

Those are Dad's words, spoken almost thirty years ago, in 1991, to faculty at Brandon University. It's appropriate to give him the first words in the story of his life—words illustrating the feeling of living on the land, and the ways of knowing and learning there. Dad was born in 1935, and for the first nine years of his life, he spent most of his time on the trapline with his family.

I've been thinking back to how I wrote about the home I grew up in. I find myself, in writing out how Dad described the place where he grew up to a group of colleagues, wanting to do better. To describe the bungalow on Queenston Street more poetically, more feelingly, with the sort of beautiful words Dad used to paint a picture of his childhood home.

"How young were you when you started to live on the trapline?" I asked.

I know his family had a house on Robertson Bay. Two of them, in fact: a newer two-storey house and a prefab bungalow they moved into after Auntie Effie burned the other down. I can't say what I'd expected Dad's response to be; I didn't think I'd hear something profound or surprising. He'd lived in a house, and at some point, when he was old enough, he had moved out onto the land. Simple. But Dad chuckled and answered as though it were self-evident.

"I was a baby."

The trapline had been his home from the beginning. That was

the way of life for Dad, his family, and many people in Norway House. They were born to the land. They had a job to do, and Dad was groomed for that job almost from the moment of his inception. He and his family would spend autumn, winter, and spring on a series of traplines. At first, their trapline was wherever they went; it was only when the federal government stepped in and began to look after things, as the government is wont to do, that land was parcelled out and people had specific traplines to call their own. They would leave for the trapline before freeze-up, and there they would stay until spring, usually May, after the ice broke. I picture Nana, nine months pregnant with Dad, on a canoe heading back to the community after spending almost her entire pregnancy on the land.

I asked Dad when the family would head up to the trapline.

"Probably around August, somewhere around there."

That meant Dad was three months old when he went for the first time, not including the months he'd been there inside Nana's womb.

"What was life like out there when you were a kid?"

"I don't remember. That's a long time ago."

I remember the silence that followed. I remember Dad sitting on the couch in my office, staring out the window—at what, I don't know. Maybe nothing. Maybe searching for something in his mind's eye, something I couldn't see, something just coming back into focus for him. The more he's thought about his past, the more memories have come back to him. In some ways, those memories were, and are, connected to the knowledge he was given during his time on the land—knowledge that was, and is, connected to the Swampy Cree language he spoke as a child. I remember the silence, and then Dad cleared his throat and turned away from the window, and the memories flowed from his mouth to my ears. As if that boy, sitting on a hill, looking out over the water, had been waiting for this moment.

THE FAMILY'S MOST important work on the land was trapping muskrats for pelts; it was how they subsisted. A trap looks kind of like a mousetrap, but for really big mice. Dad drew one for me once. It was made of metal, a chain attached to it, and fastened to a branch or something of the sort. The trap would be partially submerged in the water, then fixed in place. There'd be a scent on it—a "stink thing," as Dad put it—to attract female muskrats. When an animal triggered the trap, it would snap shut and the animal would drown.

Trappers would pull the pelts off the animals in one motion so that the skin remained fully intact. It looked like a mitt, Dad said. The skin would be inside out and left that way to dry. They would preserve the meat to be consumed through the winter months. Other animals were also caught. At a young age, Dad learned how to set snares for rabbits. The wapos, or rabbit, was strictly for eating; its pelt wasn't worth anything. There were partridges, ducks, geese, and if you had the time and inclination, you might find and kill a moose. This would feed everybody on the trapline for a long time. No food was taken out to the trapline from the community. If you were hungry, you caught something. If you didn't catch something, you went hungry. It was a beautifully simple life.

WRITING ABOUT THIS process of hunting doesn't bother me. One of the things I hear repeatedly is that a vegan will always tell you he or she is vegan. Apparently, we vegans are quick to get into a discussion about ethics. I guess that's true; I've seen that sort of proud admission, and the subsequent discussion, or argument, take place in person and on social media. I've been teased about my dietary choice, in good nature, mostly when I'm in First Nations communities. A family friend who has since passed on, Victor Harper, teased me the best. He lived in Wasagamack, a community on the western shore of Island Lake. I went up there with Dad a few years ago for a community feast. I'm used to going into First Nations communities and finding very little I can eat, so I generally take my own food (or more accurately, Jill reminds me to take my own food). But I'm still in the habit of checking to see what else I can eat other than veggie meat. It's almost always just mixed vegetables and berries. That night in Wasagamack, I was standing in front of long tables set end to end to end and looking over the food that had been prepared. It was mostly wild meat.

Victor came to stand with me. "David, do you know there's a word for you in my language?"

"No," I said. "What is it?"

I was genuinely interested. Over the too few years I knew Victor, I cherished our talks. He was a staunch believer in the value of language revitalization. He believed it was vital for young people to become language keepers in order to preserve the many Indigenous cultures, and he knew how important land-based education is in the development of a child. A brilliant man with a gentle wit.

"I don't think you'd understand the word in the Island Lake dialect," he admitted, "but it translates roughly to 'bad hunter.'"

I'd heard this joke before from Indigenous People, and once—far less funny—from a non-Indigenous person. Victor delivered it with the timing of a professional comedian.

I am vegan, and yes, it has become an ethical choice. Several years ago, I ran a federal workforce development program for

Indigenous People entering the manufacturing industry, and one of the workplaces I helped place students at was an animal processing plant in Brandon. The students and I toured the kill floor one day, and it was one of the most awful things I've ever seen. I don't believe in slaughtering animals like that, but I love and respect the traditional and contemporary Indigenous ways of living. I understand this way of life has historically involved snaring, hunting, fishing, and trapping. I also am aware that these animals are honoured and respected, and that's the distinction.

I'VE HEARD THE term "Indian time" a lot in my life. Once, at an old job, two white employees complained to my manager that I was taking long lunches. "He's on Indian time," they told him, a slur that was later repeated to me. Over the years, I've learned not to let these casual, or malicious, comments bother me. They are a product of ignorance. If they're said, they're believed, and if they're believed, then somebody, at some point, failed in the job we have to educate one another. This Indian time thing, I don't think there's any truth to it the way the term is commonly used. I don't think it means that as a Cree man, I'm unreliable, that I'm prone to arrive late to work or come back late from lunch. Dad's always been early for everything, and so have I. Indian time is a thing, though—it's just far less offensive, far more profound, as I've come to understand how it pertains to life in community.

Time works differently in places like Norway House. There isn't the rush you feel in the city. We're living in an age of anxiety for several reasons, but one of them, it seems to me, is that we've come to expect and want everything *right now*. We work too hard and rest too little. We are slaves to time. It is a commodity, like so many other things. To quote the futurist Ray Kurzweil, time would become meaningless if there were too much of it. We hoard it, do our best to monopolize it. But in community, nobody is in a rush. The days are languid, and so are the people. It doesn't mean they fit into the stereotype of the lazy Indian; it just means they take time to breathe.

On the trapline, time works different still. Dad and his family worked, but they weren't bound to what we would describe as regular working hours. There was no set schedule. You went out early in the morning to check the traps, then came home when you were done, when the traps had been checked and the animals collected. At home base, you'd skin the animals, prepare the meat.

"I tell people this," Dad said, "in terms of time. It was important because the animals have patterns. If you miss those patterns, like the muskrat run in the spring, then you're not going to get as many furs or eat as much. Work is like that in a way, even though it's different in the city. If you're late, then you've missed something."

FAMILIES WENT ONTO the trapline together and stayed together over the harsh winter months to look after one another. They were a large extended family. For the Robertsons, the people they stayed with on the land were relatives, many through traditional adoption. Unlike a Western adoption, which can be a private affair, Indigenous traditional adoption is grounded in the belief that the care of a child is a communal responsibility. At times, an adoption takes place after the loss of a family member—my auntie Eleanor adopted Murray Sinclair, now a senator and formerly the chair of the Indian Residential Schools Truth and

Reconciliation Commission, after the death of her son, Tony. It's how the Sinclairs are connected to us. *Tāpākōmākan*: a person who takes the place of a deceased relative. Murray's son Niigaan isn't just a friend—he's my cousin. We aren't blood relatives, but to us there is no distinction.

On the second trapline Dad lived on, the Robertsons stayed with David Chubb and Kenneth Apetagon and their families. Both of these families are related to ours because after Nana's mother and father died, she and her brother, Henry George, were adopted into them. We became their family, they ours. For the last few years, I've wanted to get my first tattoo, a Swampy Cree word in syllabics: *niwakomakanak*. My relatives. This strikes me as an idea, like time, that means something different to Indigenous People. The concept of relatives, what it means to be a member of a family, of a community. It's why I wanted to get my Indian status. Not because I wanted slightly cheaper gas, but because I wanted to be a Norway House Cree Nation band member. It means a lot to me, just as I am sure it meant a lot to the Robertsons, the Chubbs, the Apetagons, to be a family living on the land together, to have the responsibility of looking after one another.

These families would be in one another's company for the eight- or nine-month stay on the land, living in rustic cabins or canvas tents depending on what trapline they were on, and experiencing few interruptions to that intimacy. Runners would come out to the trapline to bring flour, tea, sugar, and lard. The few things the trapline couldn't offer. They would provide these items on credit, and the family would settle up in the spring. The job of the runner, an employee of the Hudson's Bay Company, was important, though the visits were infrequent. Runners would come out only in the winter, by dog sled, and there was no set schedule for their arrival.

On the trapline, everybody had a job, none more important than another. Men would spend the days checking their traps, resetting them if necessary, collecting the game. They got up early in the morning and returned whenever the job was done. The women's job on the trapline was the same as the women's job at home. They would keep the home base in good order, look after the tent or cabin, take care of the children. But they could also often be found setting snares, skinning animals, preserving meat. I feel slightly uncomfortable talking about roles that are gender-specific, but this is the truth that lies in tradition and the way things were. I would hazard a guess, however, that as much as women contributed to the work of men, men didn't return the favour.

Dad had jobs when he was old enough. As a toddler, he of course wouldn't go out with the men to check traps, set them, and so on. But at a very young age, he was given responsibilities and taught that everyone contributes. As a child no older than seven, he was given one trap to set by the river. By the time he was a teenager, that one trap had grown to many, and he recalls catching forty muskrats during one seasonal spring run. There was an important development process under way; Elders paid careful attention during these formative years to fostering the role of provider. The honour of being given a trap as a child led my father to catch all forty of those muskrats years later.

Dad remembers chopping wood often, as soon as the adults were sure that he could perform the task without hurting himself. He'd help gather and then change the spruce boughs that served as mattresses. My family and I often camp over the summer, opting to stay in tents rather than hotels when we go on long trips—four years ago to Haida Gwaii, last year to Nova Scotia. We sleep on air mattresses. I can't imagine sleeping on spruce boughs, but Dad has assured me they were just as good. They were soft, he told me, and more than that, they smelled nice. He'd fall asleep to their scent. Air mattresses smell like hot breath and plastic, and in my experience, they end up deflated more often than inflated due to errant holes. Score one for nature.

If you head north on the water, away from Norway House, you'll follow a series of rivers and lakes that embrace small islands and are surrounded by forest. The water is dotted with beaver dams, the trees with eagle nests. You'll see something glittering out of the corner of your eye, turn your head, and catch a muskrat disappearing under the water. Eventually, you'll come to a body of water where there is a line under the surface. On one side of the line, the water is a shade of blue; on the other, near midnight black. On the land a short distance west, no more than fifty meters, there's a clearing that slopes up towards the forest. In the middle of this clearing rests a boulder that's as black as the water on the other side of the line. As black as obsidian. This is Black Water. A trapline and, at one time, a gathering place. Families would congregate there at the beginning of trapping season, then branch off towards their own lines, only to come together once more in the spring.

"I remember a little bit about Black Water," Dad said. "Pieces."

The river continues on from there, carves a path through the land, branches off into smaller tributaries that lead ever deeper into the bush, farther away from the community. Somewhere across Hairy Lake, northeast of Black Water and through a thin river just wide enough for a canoe, was the trapline Dad remembers more clearly. Ironically, though, he can't find the way there. How odd, I thought, to know a place so well, but for that place to be lost to the past. I want to find it one day. Map the way there so it's not lost again.

There was a little log cabin on the treeline that might still be there today. It was shared by my family, the Chubbs, and the Apetagons. The last few years Dad went out to the trapline, he went there. By then, it was just him and his father, and they'd go out together in the spring for the muskrat run, remaining in Norway House for the rest of the year. Dad remembers the cabin. He remembers the cabin, and he remembers the water. He misses the water, not the cabin. He misses being near the water.

The Robertsons have a different sort of journey these days, a trip to southern Manitoba's Riding Mountain National Park, ending in Wasagaming. There's a place there called Thunderbird Bungalows that I've stayed at since I was a child. My family, Cam's family, sometimes Mike's family, Mom and Dad—we go there every August for one week. It's a short walk to Clear Lake. That's why Dad, in particular, likes Wasagaming so much: because the water is so near. There's a bench on the pier where you can sit and just be. He likes to sit on that bench.

"But it's not just the water—it's being outside."

Maya, my oldest niece, goes on canoe trips every year, away from her family for two weeks. Dad tells her, "Listen to the wind, and it will talk to you." There's something peaceful about the water and the air and the land, and the wind *does* speak to you. It gives you a sense of peace. That's why people are so calm when they're on the land, cradled within the arms of Mother Earth.

When Dad left the trapline for the last time, he didn't know that he wouldn't return for many years, and that absence changed him. It changed his entire family. You could still live the same sort of life at home—it wasn't that. Nearly everything you did on the trapline, you could do around the community. You could set snares, hunt prairie chickens. In the summer, Dad would swim and make paper freighters, pretending that he, like his father, was working on them. He'd make tiny propellers so the paper boats would create little waves and look like real boats. Eventually, when he was older, Dad would go duck shooting with his adopted brother, Allan. But the need to support the family from the land disappeared, not because the demand for pelts fell away, but because the government started a social assistance program in the mid-1940s. Families who'd lived on traplines opted for a government allowance instead. You hunted, trapped, and snared because you wanted to eat wild meat, not because you were hungry, not because you needed to bring pelts to the Hudson's Bay Company for money. If you went out to hunt food and came home empty-handed, it didn't matter. You hunted to eat what you traditionally ate, but if you didn't catch anything, you could buy some Klik at the store.

On the land, it mattered. There was the water and the wind and the land and the stars. There were ways to tell the weather. Dad told me that his classroom was Mother Earth. You didn't have chairs and desks, blackboards and teachers. You had a tree stump, stories, and a grandparent. The way you learned was different, but you learned. You learned things just as well, and I would argue with greater importance, because if you didn't learn, you wouldn't survive. That's just the way it was *kayās*, long ago. That's just the way they used live.

There was a place across from Norway House. In the spring, when trappers were ready to head back to the community from the land, people set up camp there to wait for them to come canoeing down the river. They would be there for a day or two, covered with the sort of peace that Dad has often talked of. Expectant but patient. Word would come to the trappers that people were gathering in Norway House, and on a given day, they would all return to the community together in their canoes. When they arrived, family and friends lined the shore to welcome them. They would see all their relations—the ones they hadn't seen for months. Aunts. Uncles. Cousins. Grandparents. There would be bannock and soup waiting for them, a celebration that they were back and had returned together.

NIKOTWASIK (SIX)

——

Dad's waiting for me when I enter the hotel. He's sitting with his legs crossed, one hand on his lap, an arm stretched over the top of the couch. He looks so relaxed that it's as if he could sink right into the cushions and disappear. When he sees me, he gets up with some effort—getting up from soft couches is laborious at his age—and we check in at the front desk. I follow him up the flight of stairs to the second floor, carrying his suitcase, and we walk to his room. I ask him to have supper with me, but he's brought food with him in a small cooler, and I can tell that he wants to be on his own. If Dad hasn't grown to love our conversations, he at least appreciates them and the time we spend together. But he likes his alone time, too, and I respect that. We make plans to meet up in the lobby after we've both eaten, and I leave him to his quiet.

I leave the hotel altogether, venture outside into the fading light. I have to because I forgot to pack any food. Sometimes I tell Jill that I can get ready for trips on my own, that I'm not one of the kids, and then things like this happen. I start towards the York Boat Diner, wondering what, if anything, they'll have for me to eat. Probably fries, maybe the house salad. And that's only if they haven't changed the menu from the previous owner's. I get halfway there, to the large rectangular hole that will one day be the community hall, when I turn away from the diner and plot a new course. I'm not that hungry anyway. Maybe it's the panic attack I had earlier, maybe it's that I'm far more excited about tomorrow than I am about fries and salad, maybe it's that I still feel nervous despite the medication and being here with Dad. Whatever it is, I head towards the water.

The air is fresh and crisp up here, different than the air I breathe in the city. It burns my nostrils in the best possible way while I cross the road, inching ever closer to Little Playgreen Lake. I breathe deeper the closer I get, and breath by breath, I become more accustomed to the air.

I turn right and begin to walk west, towards the old United Church and the land that best overlooks the water, the place where, in July, at the cliff's edge, there's a perfect view of the York boat races. That's where I want to be—a spot where I can see almost the entire community.

On my first trip to Norway House, we drove to where the York boats launch. We were going to get out of our rented vehicle and stand by the water together as a family. It was nighttime and the moon was reflecting off the lake's surface. The stars were countless. It was a perfect moment and a perfect place to be together, but then our headlights revealed a pack of large rez dogs right in front of our van, their eyes glowing menacingly. Norway

House, like most other First Nations communities, has its share
of rez dogs. They're along the roads, in the gravel driveways of
prefab houses, outside of grocery stores, following you around
wanting attention. While they were new to me on my first trip to
a community, they aren't anymore. Typically they're friendly. You
can tell by looking at them. Their big eyes, their tongues wag-
ging out of their mouths like second tails. These dogs, staring us
down through the glare of the headlights, were not. That perfect
moment would have to wait for another day. We reversed the van
and left the water's edge.

That was my first time in Rossville. And though I've now
driven through it a number of times, I've never walked. I find
my way to the church by following the roadside like any other
band member walking to or from the mall. It makes me feel
even more like I belong here, a "when in Rome" kind of thing.
I wave at people as they pass by, on foot or in vehicles. They
wave back. I wonder how many people recognize me as my
father's son. The roads wind around the community, and I have
to pay attention or I'll turn the wrong direction and head away
from the water rather than towards it. I've done that in the car,
despite the many times I've been here. This makes me feel less
like I belong.

I arrive at the old church and walk around the perimeter of
the structure. It was built decades ago by Joe Keeper, a veteran of
the First World War and member of the 1912 Olympic team (his
fourth-place finish is still Canada's best result in the 10,000-metre
race). A carpenter by trade, Joe built the church meticulously.
It's not been used as a church for years—the front door is always
padlocked whenever I've come here over the last ten years—but
the exterior of it looks in perfect condition, aside from peeling
white paint up the steeple. One lap, at times running my hand

along the surface, then I continue on to the edge of the land, beside a memorial cairn for James Evans, the reverend for whom the church is named.

I stand there, looking over the lake, over the community beyond and around it, trying to find Robertson Bay, where Dad lived after his time on the trapline, trying to picture him and his siblings swimming in the cool waters. I stand there and do what Dad has told Maya—and me—to do: listen to the wind and the water it pushes towards the shore in tiny waves. That same wind feels cool against my skin. Fresh. Crisp.

I leave the water and walk slowly back to the hotel, my hands in my pockets, enjoying the unique northern quiet. The rest of the evening passes deliberately. Dad and I are apart and then together as the sky begins to darken, bringing us closer, each moment, to tomorrow. We're really just passing time. We walk to the mall in the twilight, moving away from the dying sun and the deep blue sky, where clouds gathering on the horizon look like a distant mountain range.

"INTO THIS PEACEFUL place came a new sound, like the whine of a persistent mosquito. You shake your head, trying to evade it, hoping it won't land in your ear, but the sound stayed. In fact, it got louder. You looked up into the sky, trying to place it. There is a moving dot, no bigger than a sparrow, making the sound. The sparrow becomes a crow. The crow becomes an airplane, with its buzz getting harsher as it circles the lake. Everybody is looking at it, this noise breaking the harmony of the pines. Like a giant dragonfly, the Canso lands on the water, the beat of the heavy motor like a backwash on the shoreline. It ploughs loudly to the community and stops, its engines sputtering into silence. This

silence mirrors the frustration already clear on the faces of the
First Nations people on the shore."

They knew why the float plane had arrived, why the quiet,
which had once meant calm, meant something different now. The
terrible anticipation of their children—some as young as six, some
younger still—who would have to board the plane and be spir-
ited away to residential school. Dad's description of the abduc-
tion stands in stark contrast to his memories of the land. Again,
he was narrating this to faculty members at Brandon University
almost thirty years ago. This time, the quiet he spoke of cast the
same sort of eerie pall over those in the crowd as it had the community; they imagined children filing onto the machine that was
once thought to be a sparrow, and being taken.

There was no other choice for parents, not after 1920. That's
when the Canadian government amended the Indian Act in an
effort to combat low attendance at the schools. Here, I think of
Chief Berens withholding his community's children from Norway House Indian Residential School because they were being fed
rotten fish and were showing signs of frostbite. He'd kept the kids
home to protect their well-being.

His wasn't the only act of defiance by Indigenous People; it
wasn't the only act of protection once parents understood the
realities of the residential school system. Understood that by
attending, their children would suffer emotional, mental, spiritual, sexual, and/or physical abuse. How was the government to
respond to this defiance?

The answer was to make school attendance compulsory to
counter those who would dare hide or withhold their children.
The Indian Act amendment gave the Indian agent the power
to simply walk into a house in a community and kidnap the
children living there. A good friend of mine, Betty Ross, was

taken in this way. She'd been adopted by a loving family in Cross Lake First Nation after getting kicked out of her house by her mother in the middle of winter. It was the kind of love she sorely needed. She and her adoptive family lived by the water, across from an unfamiliar building, dark and cold in appearance. One day, there came a moving dot, which, as it drew closer, revealed itself to be a priest in a canoe. This man in a dark robe came to the shore and, without a word to her adoptive parents, took Betty by the hand and forced her into the canoe. All her mother and father could do was watch. Often, these abductions would take place with the help of law enforcement. Parents who tried to shield their children from inevitable pain risked imprisonment.

"Any parent, guardian or person with whom an Indian child is residing," the amendment stated, "who fails to cause such child, being between the ages aforesaid, to attend school as required by this section after having received three days notice so to do by a truant officer shall, on the complaint of the truant officer, be liable on summary conviction before a justice of the peace or Indian agent to a fine of not more than two dollars and costs, or imprisonment for a period not exceeding ten days or both, and such child may be arrested without a warrant and conveyed to school by the truant officer."

In 1944, the year Dad left the trapline as a way of life, this amendment to the Indian Act was still in force, and he was of an age when he would have been subject to it. Ironically, though, it was the Canadian government's own process for determining who was an Indian by law that saved him from having to attend the residential school in Norway House.

My great-grandfather, John Charles Wesley Robertson, was Scottish. When my great-grandmother, Sarah Jane (the same name as Nana), who was full-blooded Cree, married John, she lost her status through enfranchisement. The purpose of enfranchisement was to assimilate Indigenous People and, ultimately, reduce the number of "Indians" for whom the Canadian government was financially responsible. As a result, James Robertson, Sarah and John's son, never had status, and when Nana, Sarah Jane Captain, married him, she lost her status just as my great-grandmother had.

It was a government-sanctioned game of dominoes, only with human beings, and the game continued when Dad was born. He wasn't a status Indian until April 1985, when Bill C-31, a further amendment to the Indian Act, passed into law. That amendment was an attempt to bring the act into line with the gender-equality provisions of the Canadian Charter of Rights and Freedoms. You see, if the roles had been reversed and my great-grandmother had been Scottish while my great-grandfather was Cree, she would have *become* a status Indian on their marriage.

But because Dad was not a status Indian at any point during his childhood, he was never required to attend residential school. If he had been, he would've left the trapline for that reason. If he'd failed to do so, Nana and my grandfather could've been fined or incarcerated. But he had no status, and therefore no need to return to the community. Why, then, would the entire family move from the trapline, where they lived happily for nine months of every year amid the calm the land offered, into the community?

The answer is that historically—and frankly, to this day— the Canadian government has had a lot of tricks up its sleeve to accomplish what it first set out to do in the late nineteenth century. This intent may best be illustrated by a quote from Duncan Campbell Scott, an accomplished poet and also the deputy superintendent of the Department of Indian Affairs from 1913 to 1932: "I want to get rid of the Indian problem . . . Our objective is to continue until there is not a single Indian in Canada that has not been absorbed into the body politic, and there is no Indian question."

The Family Allowance, Canada's first universal welfare program, proved to be another example of systemic racism within a colonial system that was structured to answer what Scott referred to as the "Indian question." Beginning in 1945, financial assistance was given without considering a family's income or assets; the idea was that all children are worthy of support. There's a lot of history behind the Family Allowance, most of it stemming from the Great Depression, but I find myself stopping at that first point. It's true, of course—all children are unquestionably worthy of support. The statement, however, assumes an equality that was far from reality for Indigenous People in 1944.

For families to receive the allowance, their children had to be under the age of sixteen and living at a permanent residence. But a trapline does not have a street address. For Indigenous parents, the question became: What do we do? While some families continued to live out on the land, forgoing the assistance in pursuit of traditional subsistence, many left the land behind. That included the Robertsons, who moved back into Norway House. After 1944, Dad would go out to the trapline with his father for the muskrat run in the spring. They would stay for a few weeks, not the better part of a year, and then return to the community. At fourteen, Dad stopped going on the land altogether, and thought he would never return.

There was one last condition that had to be met for families to qualify for benefits offered by the government: not only did children have to be under sixteen and living at a permanent residence, but they also had to be enrolled in school. So at the age of nine, Dad, whose lessons had always come from the land, went into the classroom.

"Everybody has their own issue," Dad said in 2019. "Mine was Family Allowance. What it did was break up the traplines for the families. Everybody else, if they wanted the allowance, they'd have to move into the community. Some families, three or four, went onto the land anyway. But it had a generational impact; we became more domesticated. There was far less freedom to our lives. And we lost the way of living on the land, and the knowledge around it."

SCHOOLS WERE SPREAD all over the surrounding area, in Norway House, Rossville, and farther south. Children designated as status Indians typically went to Norway House Indian Residential School or one of five federally run day schools (Playgreen School, Jack River A.C. School, Nickaway R.C. Day School, Towers Island, and Jack River R.C. Day School). Non-status children like Dad went to one of at least four public schools. Dad was enrolled in one near Robertson Bay, locally referred to as the Old School, until sixth grade, when he transferred to the North School. The North School was across the road from the Fort, and Dad was there for the last two years of his education. All of the area's schools, federally run or otherwise, went only to grade eight.

The Old School was close enough to Robertson Bay that you could see it from the family home. Robertson Bay is a piece of land that swells out into Little Playgreen Lake, and the school was on a similar type of land formation, near where an RCMP detachment now stands. It was a one-room building with two-seat benches, and there was a schoolyard outside. But it was just that: a yard. No play structure, no slide, no swings. In the classroom, traditional subjects were taught: reading, writing, and arithmetic. Each of these subjects was new to Dad. He'd never read a book before. Had never touched pencil to page. Had never solved a math equation. These simple facts alone made school very difficult for him and his classmates, many of whom had also recently settled into a permanent residence so their families could qualify for social assistance. To make matters worse, Dad spoke no English; he only spoke Swampy Cree. He had to learn English as much as he had to learn the subjects. Or rather, he had to learn English in order to learn the subjects at all. As he put it, "You were fluent in a language you couldn't use, and all the knowledge you brought into the classroom was useless."

The schools Dad attended differed in many ways from the residential schools and federally run day schools, but they had similarities as well. Most notably, a child was not permitted to speak his or her language, Swampy Cree, in the school building or the schoolyard. "They couldn't fully control us, though," Dad said, "so we used to speak Cree to each other in the bush."

But they couldn't stay in the bush forever. They could no longer live there for months at a time, speaking only their language, learning from the land. At the time, they perhaps weren't as mindful of the impact this had. They were living in a vastly different way than they had lived before. Going to school. And they were learning there, of course, but learning different things, with a different delivery, and in a different language. On the land, the only time they heard an English word was when it stumbled off the clumsy tongue of the runner who brought food over the winter. Otherwise, everything they knew, they learned in Swampy Cree. And they learned a lot. Then they started school and switched languages, and all those things they knew—all those things they'd learned—fell unceremoniously to the wayside.

Thirty years ago, Dad wrote a paper about his first day at school titled "Speaking in Tongues." The paper, written by Dad years after he'd become a key figure in Indigenous education both in Manitoba and throughout Canada, was intended to influence educational reform. It read, in part:

> *I walked into the small building, where my friends and relatives were sitting, full of confidence and courage. The young people were sitting in neat rows on wooden seats and [at] small tables. They were quiet and attentive, much like my father and grandfather behaved when they were stalking animals. The door opened to the building and a small, untanned person walked into the room, walked in front of everybody and began to speak in tongues. (This is a term I learned later in life.) She was very confident and commanded respect from the young people, and some of the young people appeared to respond in the same strange sounds she was making. I was nine years old, an adult in the eyes of my people, and I did not understand the words she was making. I became very scared and insecure. In one brief session, in the small one-room classroom, I had lost confidence and became confused about the learning situation.*
>
> *I was told to come to this house and be taught and I couldn't understand one word the teacher was saying;*

*my desire to learn turned to fear. She was teaching
in English, and I only understood Cree . . . I am told
Education means to "draw out," that the first prin-
ciple in teaching is to start from the known and work
towards the unknown. What did the teacher who was
teaching when I first entered a school know about my
known? The materials which the teacher used were in
her language, using examples taken from her world
and the experience of her people. The known in my
world was the experience and the language of the Cree
people.*

Dad went on to make two main arguments in the paper. First,
he suggested that teacher training programs prepare educators to
work with Indigenous children by emphasizing that they teach
from the known and work towards the unknown. That is to say,
they should connect with students based on *the students'* world-
view, not the teacher's. So if that small, untanned person had
stridden to the front of the one-room schoolhouse and taught the
Indigenous children from an understanding of their lived experiences, acknowledging that they had already learned a great deal
while living on the land, the situation would have been more positive and effective. Second, he insisted that the same consideration
be given to Indigenous students as was given to francophone students. If we can teach French students in French, recognizing
the importance of their language and culture to their identity,
why can't we do the same with Indigenous kids? Why can't a
Cree student be taught in Cree? If one plus one equals two, is it
not acceptable that *pēyak* plus *pēyak* equals *nīso*? I'm simplifying
Dad's argument here, but the sentiment is as important as the
inequity is undeniable.

Dad's own experiences of school had left him feeling as if he were being pulled in two directions. One moment he was running off into the bush to speak Swampy Cree with his friends, and the next he was working hard to learn English so he could excel in his studies. Surely, this work ethic was encouraged by his mother, who knew that he had to be educated to find success in a changing world. That change was no more evident than when the family moved into the community permanently.

Dad did succeed. By the time he'd reached grade seven and had moved on to the North School, an institution built close to the Hudson's Bay Company fort, he was fluent in English. In eighth grade, he was an excellent student in all the main subjects. His favourite was reading. When Dad told me this, I wasn't surprised. He remains a voracious reader of all types of books, fiction and non-fiction, contemporary and historical, self-help and motivational, academic, cultural (he has a wide selection of Cree literature), and so on. But success came at a cost, as it usually does.

The cost of his success is something I can feel today. It is one of the reasons why my brothers and I were never raised to speak Swampy Cree. Language loss has been, arguably, the most profound impact of any system established to educate Indigenous children. To use a simple equation: language = culture.

The way Indigenous People communicated with each other in communities began to change when the schools were established. The express intent of the schools was to teach Indian children the ways of the dominant white society for their betterment. To, as the infamous phrase goes, kill the Indian in the child. From my own experience and what I've learned through conversations I've had with Dad over the years, I know that Indigenous children did, in fact, learn things. Dad *did* learn mathematics. He *did* learn how to read. He *did* learn how to write. But Indigenous children were *not* taught that they could have had their education and kept their language at the same time. And kept their intrinsic value as Indians. It was what Dad argued for in the early 1990s: bilingual education. The truth that *pēyak* plus *pēyak* equals *nīso* is as valid as one plus one equals two.

Back then, nobody knew anything about that. Nobody understood that not knowing the English names for things didn't invalidate what a child knew in Swampy Cree. The fact that Dad didn't know *moshom* was "grandpa" in English didn't make Moshom *not* Grandpa. Still, instead of *moshom* meaning "grandpa," Moshom became Grandpa.

Dad explained it this way: "If I see a book and say, 'This is a book,' that would have been a new concept for me entirely. I wouldn't have known what a book was. There might've been books around, sure, but certainly not for teaching me anything. So almost everything that I knew, every single thing, had a different name. As a result, we, as Cree children, had to translate our knowledge into a new language. But the thing was, we didn't know that language. What was English? The easiest thing was just to learn the new language by leaving our language behind."

Moshom became "grandpa." *Masinahikan* became "book." *Wakomakanak* became "relatives." *Aspin* became "gone." Et cetera.

I WAS NINE years old, an adult in the eyes of my people.

That line from Dad's paper struck me when I first read it, and it has remained with me since. My youngest daughter, Lauren, just turned nine. She's a powerful Indigenous girl; I know that she will help change this country. I have an unwavering faith in children, but when I look at her, I still see a kid. She has said and done things that have left Jill and me in awe. We found out a year and a half ago that she has no depth perception, and yet she'd been doing gymnastics—the balance beam, the parallel bars, climbing the rope to the ceiling. She and two other friends started a Kids Who Care Club at her school; students from all grades, kindergarten to eight, are invited to come and talk about ways in which they can make the world a better place. The first meeting attracted thirty-five kids from a relatively small student population. She does something every day that makes me think, makes me *know*, she's wise beyond her years. But she's in grade three, and it will be years before I see her as an adult. Life was different for Dad on the trapline. The things he learned, the responsibilities he had. By Lauren's age, he was setting traps and snares. He was catching muskrats and rabbits. He was participating in his family's subsistence. Lauren tells us that she's going to get a job soon to help pay for groceries (having five kids does put a strain on expenses), but I think we're going to hold off on that for a few years.

"I LIE TO people," Dad said. "I say that I was six feet, two hundred pounds when I was nine years old."

He felt that way. He felt bigger than his age. An adult in the eyes of his people. And then, suddenly, as soon as he sat down for class in that one-room schoolhouse, he was a boy who knew nothing, whose knowledge held little value.

Dad has struggled for decades with the knowledge that was lost. He has been talking about it more often these days. Reaching back through the years to the time he was a child, with the benefit of hindsight, and trying to recapture it. He told me that no matter how young they are, kids aren't empty vessels. They have a great amount of knowledge accumulated through their lived experiences, whether on the land or in a meeting with other kids who want to do something good in their community. Dad was not an empty vessel, and neither were the other kids in his class. He, too, carried a lot of knowledge when he arrived at school, but it was only recently, more than seventy years removed from his first day, that he recognized he could use that knowledge. That the things he knew that made him an adult in the eyes of his people were not lost. That the things he had known could be rediscovered. I think this realization has come as he's grown more aware of his own mortality, and he is rediscovering the knowledge not to keep for himself but to pass down to future generations. His children. His children's children.

He has been finding Cree knowledge once thought lost by recommitting himself to the language and the act of remembering. He has learned to translate what he knew in Swampy Cree to English. He has come to understand that learning English did not negate what he knew before, and he has spent a significant amount of time since that life-changing epiphany remembering—and through the act of remembering, reclaiming.

There is a recliner in Dad's office, my old bedroom. The chair is too comfortable, if you ask me. Sometimes when I visit Mom and Dad, he's sleeping in it, the foot rest raised up, the back lowered down. Earphones serenading him with classical music. Other times, he's sitting there, staring out the window into the vastness of the sky, at nothing and everything all at once, and I know that he's taking the time to remember because the Cree knowledge is there for him now—values, beliefs, traditions, ways of living. Teachings that at one point existed only in Swampy Cree, but that he has learned to understand in English. Knowledge that goes back a long way, to time immemorial. When Dad sits in the chair and stares out the window, he's trying to think back on the way he lived and ask himself questions. What is that knowledge? How can he remember it, reclaim it, so that it becomes useful to him once more? How can it be passed on to the next generation, to ensure its legacy?

"When language programs work, they work really well," Dad said. "Kids can use the knowledge that they brought with them, rather than believe they have to abandon it." Dad abandoned the knowledge he'd been gifted on the land in favour of the English language because he believed that there wasn't a better way, that the knowledge existed only within the Swampy Cree dialect, within the Cree culture. When he was just a young boy, not much older than my youngest son, James, Dad and his grandfather spent an afternoon fishing. Out of the fish they caught, they prepared one to eat as a reward for their hard work. The rest would be saved for family and friends, which was the way things were. The fish was cooked, and when it was ready, his grandfather put it onto a flat piece of rock.

"Aren't we going to use plates?" Dad asked.

His grandfather chuckled and shook his head. He told Dad that they didn't need plates because Creator had been cleaning the rock for thousands of years just for him to eat off. This was a teaching at once simple and profound. This teaching had been lost for decades, only to be rediscovered in the twilight of Dad's life and told to me. My job is to tell my children. Recently, I did just that; I recounted the story to Lauren and asked what she thought it meant. She paused thoughtfully, then said, "That it doesn't matter. Don't judge a book by its cover." These teachings were a gift, a gift Dad is now able to recall.

When he turned eighty, he began to speak about the importance of grandparents and the vital role they had in not only passing on their knowledge to the coming generations, but also aiding children in their journey to hold that knowledge in their hearts so tightly that it can't be lost. Dad began to use the word "grandparents" in place of "Elders," and unsurprisingly, he focused his work almost entirely on what grandparents have to offer their grandchildren. So children can carry the knowledge with them in their language, rather than believe they have to abandon it.

Some things have not changed, which means we have a lot of work to do. Dad knows that his work isn't done yet either, even if it does involve staring out the window. (When staff members came into his office to find him sitting quietly at his desk, he used to joke that he was paid to think.) His best friend, Strini Reddy, called him a visionary in a recent interview, and from all I know about Dad, that's an accurate description. But the plans he had for Indigenous education—the ideas he wrote about in the early 1990s and even before that in other articles and essays, and has worked towards for over forty years—are, by and large, still waiting to be completed. Why? If the role of education truly is to "draw out," if the role of an educator is to work from the known and move into the unknown, why do we continue to do things in opposition to this reality? And how does it benefit Indigenous youth? Why *aren't* we showing the same consideration to Indigenous cultures that we do to French culture? It's been almost thirty years since Dad wrote "Speaking in Tongues," and I've yet to see many Cree immersion schools. Starting from the known not only prepares kids for the unknown, the world they might not yet understand, but also ensures that *their* known isn't forgotten. That new experiences don't eliminate what the kids have already experienced because it's not valued enough, or as much. It ensures that they can keep their known no matter where their paths take them, and it might even help them find their way.

TĒPAKOHP (SEVEN)

The mall is a hotspot each time I visit. The large parking lot is busy even at dusk. The majority of vehicles in the lot are trucks or vans. There are other vehicles lined up along the front of the building for pickups, and a crowd of people loiter around the entrance waiting for their rides. A number of rez dogs mix in with the crowd, ambling from one person to the next, begging for food. They don't often come away empty-handed; at the very least, they'll get a friendly pat on the head, if not a bit of jerky or a chip or a French fry. Dad and I walk through the parking lot and along the line of vehicles, then navigate the throng of community members and dogs. We go inside.

Dad sits and waits for me at one of the tables in Tim Hortons, black coffee in hand, visiting with whomever he comes across as though he never left the community. I wander the Northern Store's aisles. There are toys, sporting goods, clothing, shoes, toiletries, diapers, non-perishable foods, chips and soft drinks, frozen foods, dairy, meat, and produce. If I didn't know any better, I might think I was in the city. Except for the prices. It's hard to understand how a small container of pineapple in Norway House could cost four times as much as it does in the city, while a bag of chips is more or less the same. Several factors contribute to the prevalence of diabetes in First Nations communities, but the fact that you are forced to choose between a large amount of unhealthy food or a few apples is a big one. I end up leaving with a bag of chips and a bottle of vitamin water, a snack after an unsatisfying dinner at the York Boat Diner.

There's a new gaming centre next door to the York Boat Inn, and we stop there before turning in for the night. Dad's not a gambler, but I've lost him to a casino once or twice. In Minneapolis one year, at Mystic Lake, an enormous space full of video lottery terminals and card tables, I couldn't find him for hours and freaked out slightly. Thankfully, this place is small: an L-shaped room that wraps around and opens into a central room with a stage and some tables and chairs. Dad's whereabouts are never a concern.

There's no entertainment tonight. Instead, over the course of an hour, the mechanical and incessant bleeping and whirring of the slots croons to us. Dad, who likes to play the traditional slot games, where you spin pictures to make matches (if there's a technical name, I don't know what it is), comes away empty-handed, down a few dollars. I've always stuck to Jacks or Better and manage to leave with thirty-seven dollars to the good after reluctantly feeding a machine a twenty. I rarely play the slots, but when I do,

I usually win something; my secret is to quit when I'm ahead. I mean, even if it's a dollar, I'm out.

By the time we leave, it's dark. Dad gets wiped out fast these days, but I'm tired too. It's a short walk to the hotel—out one door and in another. We climb the stairs to the second floor, and I chaperone him to his room. By the time I reach my own room, the same one I stayed in months ago, I'm sure that he's already asleep. Maybe he tried to finish the crossword puzzle, but his eyes gave out on him. Or turned the television on, to the one channel that comes in clearly, and watched about one second of a show.

It was a good day, as much as it was tiring. As soon as Dad walked into the airport, it was good. I cherish the time we spend together, not only because he's eighty-three but also because he's my best friend, and I love being around him for the sake of being around him. I enjoyed having a one-sided crossword competition with him over the drone of the twin-engine plane; I enjoyed helping him up the slope on the tarmac at the airport and feeling his bony hand squeeze my arm for support; I enjoyed listening to him talk to Kyle on the way into Rossville; I enjoyed walking with him across the road to the mall and watching him sip his coffee at Tim Hortons, unreservedly content.

I hope tomorrow is everything it needs to be for Dad, as he returns home, really home, for the first time in seventy years. I hope it's everything *I* need it to be, for me and for us, in seeing where Dad was raised. Before I drift to sleep, I realize that the anxiety attack I had earlier wasn't from something that had happened before, but from a fear that my expectations wouldn't be met. What would that mean for all the work Dad and I have done to get to where we are now? What would that mean for all the work we have ahead? Mercifully, the day relents.

MY OLDEST SON, Cole, finished grade eight this year. He's grown a lot, shooting past Jill, who's in denial that both he and our sixteen-year-old daughter are taller than her. I'm six-foot-four, and at five ten, Cole's got a long way to go before we're eye to eye. But I still have to contend with the reality that he's very likely stronger than I am at the moment (he's training for hockey tryouts in the fall), and we can wear each other's shoes. Come September, he'll be in grade nine, starting high school. Kids grow up fast. My wife and I have tried, in vain, to slow down time so these things don't happen as quickly, but it continues to barrel forward without consideration.

Dad was fourteen when he completed grade eight. I'm not certain of his height and weight at that age, but I don't think he was six feet, two hundred pounds, as he likes to tell people. He doesn't remember what his shoe size was, but I know that we have never been able to swap footwear. He didn't attend high school in Norway House Cree Nation because the community didn't have high school. Grade eight was the end of the road. If an Indigenous kid living on reserve wanted to pursue further education, he had to leave his family, his home, his community.

Dad was content to leave his education where it was for the time being, and immediately after graduation, he started work at the Fort, splitting and piling wood. The sort of hard labour that suggests Dad was very likely strong. While Cole works out in a gym, my father was by the river, lining up pieces of wood and chopping them in half with an axe, one after the other, all day long, day after day. Then he'd make large piles out of the halved wood. It reminds me of the training montage in *Rocky IV*, when Rocky heads over to the then Soviet Union to fight Ivan Drago, after Drago kills Apollo Creed in the ring. Drago trains in a state-of-the-art facility, while Rocky works out in a barn or climbs mountains in knee-deep snow.

The Hudson's Bay Company store was right beside the Fort; today it's one of two Northwest Company stores in the community. Eventually, Dad stopped splitting and piling wood and started to fill shelves as a stock boy. Then he became a cashier, a position he held for around two years, until he was sixteen. At that point, he transferred to the Rossville store and worked there doing the same job.

This move, to the more densely populated area of Norway House, would prove to be important for Dad because it's how he got to know all the community people. In the 1940s, when Dad lived there, Robertson Bay was not a part of the reserve, and his contact with band members was limited to people he knew from school. The Hudson's Bay Company store in Rossville was in the heart of the reserve, near the old church.

The move also brought him to the church, literally and figuratively. This is not to say that up until then, Dad had never heard of Christianity. His paternal grandfather, John Charles Wesley Robertson—Johnny, to those who knew him—was Scottish and a diehard Methodist. All he talked about was hellfire and brimstone. Dad's understanding of Christianity from this perspective was: if you're not good, you're going to burn in hell. It was kind of terrifying. On the other hand, the man after whom Dad was named, Donald (Dulas) Alexander McIvor, a close family friend and head of a devoutly religious family of his own, would encourage Bible readings and recitations of the Lord's Prayer, no fire and brimstone in sight. Unsurprisingly, because of these two opposing views, Dad didn't really understand Christianity; he was confused by it and knew it just as a practice.

I thought I knew why Norway House Cree Nation was Christianized, because the same thing happened to many First Nations communities: missionaries came and "saved" the Indians from their primitive traditions and pagan beliefs. Everything in Norway House lines up to support this. The reserve is located near the junction of several water routes, and as a result, it was a hub of the Hudson's Bay Company fur trade and supply lines, as well as an administrative centre for Rupert's Land. No fewer than three fur-trading posts were built in the area, one of which was the Fort. The fur trade was a commercial enterprise that, among other things, financed missionary work and helped establish the colonial relationship between Western society and Indigenous People. If a reserve was on a trade route, as Norway House was, it was likely to be targeted by missionaries who sought to convert Indigenous People to the Christian religion and "save" them.

But it's not my intention to wrest agency away from the community, and I'd be remiss to disregard a dissenting view to my theory. In talking about the arrival of Christianity in Norway House and its eventual impact on his own life, Dad explained it as a situation of the community's own making, not an unwanted intrusion. Not something that happened against the will of the people. He told me that they had heard about Christianity, understood it, and wanted to know more. To obtain that knowledge, they went looking for a minister. It's likely this was James Evans, a Methodist missionary ordained as a Wesleyan minister in 1833 and the man for whom the church was named. Evans was given authority over Norway House Cree Nation in 1840, and the community served as his final resting place upon his death in 1846.

Several people had a significant impact on Dad's journey towards the Christian faith, especially those he met after starting work in Rossville, and leaders within the church community. One of the latter was Walter Keeper, who, as it turns out, was also family. Walter had taken Nana in after her father passed away. Nana became a part of the Keeper family, and my father did too. So much so that Dad called Walter his grandfather. On his mother's side, Walter was the only grandfather Dad ever knew, and he often visited and stayed with the Keeper family.

Walter Keeper was a lay minister in the United Church and preached in the afternoons, when the service was in Cree. One afternoon he was running late, and when he arrived at the church, he ran right up to the pulpit, sweaty and out of breath. He placed his Cree Bible down and frantically opened it, desperate to start the sermon because the congregation had been waiting. The Cree Bible was enormous—much larger than the English version. Of all the pages Walter could've opened to, he landed on the one on which his sermon was based. "Jesus Christ," he said, stunned by his luck. "A bull's eye!" There were two other services that day, but I bet they were far less entertaining. In the mornings, sermons were conducted by the minister, and the congregation typically consisted of non–First Nations people from the other end of the community. The evening services were a mixture of Cree and English, depending on who attended and who was available to deliver the sermon.

Walter's involvement in the church extended beyond the physical boundaries of the quaint white structure on the point that overlooks Little Playgreen Lake. He visited people all over the community and prayed with them regularly. Dad tagged along on one such visit. They were canoeing on the river, and when people saw Walter coming, they began to gather around a large rock on the shoreline. Walter steered the canoe over to them, and right then and there, he talked to them about Christianity. An impromptu sermon about the new life the religion promised. When the lesson was over, he and Dad pushed off from the shore and paddled back into the river. "You know," Walter said, "that was just like what Jesus did when he walked to the people on the water."

Dad spoke affectionately, with great respect and admiration, about Walter Keeper and the time he spent with him. His own approach to ministry was influenced by Walter; he aspired to have the same kind of impact that his grandfather had.

Walter walked in both worlds. Not only was the man a well-respected lay minister, but he was also recognized as what we Indigenous People call an Elder today. A spiritual man in the community, a keeper of knowledge. Somebody who could convey the practices and ways of living of the Cree people. He was, as well, an herbal healer. When the hospital gave up on people, they would call on Walter, and he would heal them with the medicines he kept hanging all over his porch. How odd to consider that in one home, Walter might've prayed with a family for an answer to some sort of physical or spiritual ailment, and in another home, he might have administered traditional medicines to offer a different kind of healing altogether. I'm left wondering if there was ever a question as to what healing he would use in a given situation. Prayer or traditional medicine? Or both? From time to time, the question must have presented itself.

Walter's practice was the religious experience Dad was first exposed to in a significant way when he developed a curiosity for Christianity and sought to learn more about it. Dad's always been that way. When he wants to know something, he reads all he can, talks to many people who have knowledge in that area, and makes endless notes in the hundreds of notepads he's kept over the years. Of course, he'd experienced the boogeyman-type approach with his grandfather, John Charles Wesley Robertson, which was more scary than anything. But John died in 1945, when Dad was only nine. I imagine that the fire-and-brimstone rhetoric stuck with him, much the same as fiends have stuck with me. It wouldn't have steered him towards Christianity, though. The truth is that nothing would have. Not John Charles Wesley Robertson, not Walter Keeper, not Donald Alexander McIvor. He was clear about that with me. "There was nothing or nobody," Dad said, "that told me, 'You should be like this,' or anything like that. It just happened. I just did it."

Still, I think it's important to discuss the pervasive impact religion has had on Indigenous communities. This is well documented. If the indoctrination wasn't happening at church-run schools, it was taking place in what could be viewed as church-run communities, where structures built to praise a Christian God enveloped people on reserve like baptismal water. I visit Indigenous communities, and in many of them, churches appear on the roadsides with the frequency of rez dogs. And like a rez dog, the church can be—the church has been—both feral and friendly.

While for Dad Christianity was, and continues to be, a positive experience, the church, in Indigenous communities, for Indigenous People, has also been viciously damaging. In Dad's case, his faith in Jesus Christ did not come at the expense of his identity as a Cree man. The same was true for others, like my departed friend Victor Harper. Faith didn't have to come at the expense of *any* Indigenous person's identity. But for every person like Dad and Victor, there were others who paid that exact cost. It reminds me, conceptually, of English supplanting Swampy Cree, of the untanned person walking to the front of the classroom and teaching from the unknown rather than the known. There was a better way. Missionaries could've preached the gospel to Indigenous People without the goal of conversion. Could've preached the benefits of following Jesus without sacrificing traditional practices and ways of living.

THIS CONVERSATION IS full of generalities, which feels somewhat counterintuitive, because I tend towards specificity. Christianity has had a negative impact on Indigenous People and their communities, but this is not an absolute; it has not always been the case. I take Dad at his word: the people of Norway House sought out a minister to work in their community, and this decision led Dad to make a choice to learn as much as he could about the religion, and eventually, to want to become a minister.

Career options were limited in Norway House, as they were in any remote community. You could only dream of becoming things that you'd heard of. Dad would never have aspired to become a movie star because he had never seen a movie. For him, the possibilities weren't endless; they were confined to the handful of professions that were visible to him—a teacher, a nurse, a minister. He mentioned these things because he'd seen these things. In doing a quick scan of my aunties and uncles, I realize there isn't a lot of diversity in their career choices. My aunts Marion and Effie and Eleanor were nurses. Uncle Cameron was an orderly. Uncle Robert worked for Canada Packers, a meat-packing company that was a big employer in the community. (Auntie Flora's husband, Uncle Oliver, worked for them too.) Auntie Olive was an educator. Dad doubled down: he was first a minister, then an educator.

At the HBC store, Dad became good friends with Jack Witty, who was a few years older than him, and it was through Jack that Dad got to know some of the religious teachers in the community, both Indigenous and non-Indigenous. There was a deacon who'd arrived not long after Dad started working in Rossville. She was a non-ordained minister named Margaret Martin, and she worked closely with young people, whom she saw as a vital audience for the teachings of the gospel. It always starts with the kids, doesn't it?

Margaret Martin was the first of several new young teachers to come to Norway House. All of these educators were high school graduates who had completed one course in education. There were five or six of them, and they ensconced themselves in the community. The young people, including Dad, who was seventeen at this time, got to know them very well. Of course, the educators weren't only teachers—they were also Christians. Through them, Dad began to learn even more about religion, and the more he learned, the more curious he became.

All those people—the young teachers, the deacon, the youth in the community—made a commitment to live a Christian life. To help set the direction of their lives, they all read a novel called *In His Steps* by a Congregationalist minister named Charles M. Sheldon. If you can picture a shirt affixed with a button that reads "WWJD," that would be an adequate synopsis of this particular work of literature. In the book, Reverend Henry Maxwell, pastor of the fictional First Church of Raymond, challenges his congregants not to do a single thing for an entire year without first asking themselves, "What would Jesus do?" The novel follows the characters as their lives are changed by the challenge.

All of these influences in my father's young life were significant, as was an intensely spiritual man named Ibbs Avery. Like

John Charles Wesley, Ibbs was a proud Scotsman. Now and again, he'd put on his kilt and parade around the community. Dad would often stay at the Avery house, and he got to know Ibbs and his views on conversion to the Christian faith—the new life, and new purpose, that Christianity offered.

"The thing that attracted me most," Dad said, "was that people could change the way they lived. They could be reborn. They could understand that this was the way they wanted to live and develop an awareness of what that means, both for themselves and for how they could share that with others. How they could influence others, just by how they chose to live."

Like many people of faith, Dad tried to have an impact on others by setting an example in how he lived his life. He wanted to make the sort of impression on others that Walter, Ibbs, and the deacon had made on him. The elders in the church recognized this and started to work with him in earnest. But there was only so much he could learn in Norway House.

At the time, there was a one-year training program for laypeople in Fort Qu'Appelle, Saskatchewan, called the Prairie Christian Training Centre. (This program is still in operation today.) Alternatively, there was Cook Christian Training School, a four-year program in Phoenix, Arizona. Under the guidance of elders in the community, Dad looked at both institutions and their programs, but in the end, there seemed to be only one choice. "Even back then," Dad said, "I realized that I was going to learn more in four years than I would in one, and that's where I decided to go."

When Dad lived on the trapline, it felt a long way from Norway House, but he'd really not gone too far. And though he had learned much on the land, in the classroom, and from elders and educators in Rossville, his life had always been in a small corner of the world. There was the community, and beyond it, the trees, the waters, the sky, and all the living things his family had once depended on to survive. Dad's corner of the world was small, but it had always felt big; there had always been so much space to live in, so much space to breathe. And then, when he was nineteen, his world got bigger than he could have ever imagined.

ĒNANĒW (EIGHT)

═══

I don't like this hotel room. There are ghosts in here, memories that have stayed with me since my last time in the community, my last time in this room, just a few months ago. I'd come up to do work, and hopefully to get in some visiting, like tracking down my auntie, who can be elusive for an Elder. I was to spend my first day at the Helen Betty Osborne Ininiw Education Resource Centre, a school for kindergarten to grade twelve, and my second day at Jack River School, which is kindergarten to grade six.

As much as I enjoy it, public speaking is tiring. At the end of the first day, I abandoned my intention to drive around the community visiting family, and instead stayed in my hotel room. I sat on the couch between the bed and window, and lazily checked my social media feeds. It was February 22, 2018.

Twitter was blowing up with the news that the jury had reached a verdict in the Raymond Cormier trial. Cormier had been accused of murdering Tina Fontaine, one of the thousands of Indigenous girls, women, and two-spirited people who've been killed or gone missing since 1980. Two weeks earlier, the man who'd shot Colten Boushie, another Indigenous youth, in the back of the head had been found not guilty by an all-white jury. He was eventually fined $3,900 for improperly storing his gun. Just $3,900 for killing a young Indigenous man. Ever since that trial, I'd been worried about the outcome of this one.

The news hit. Not guilty.

I remember sitting there, frozen. I couldn't feel my heart. Maybe it had shattered to pieces inside my chest. I started crying. Suddenly, I had no idea what to say to all the kids in Jack River School the next day. It was my dear friend Cherie Dimaline, the author of *The Marrow Thieves*, who advised me to tell them that they mattered and were loved. So class by class, I did just that, whether they knew what had happened or not. Because one day they would know, and like many Indigenous People in Canada at the time, they would wonder if their lives mattered. Imagine having to muse about your worth. Shouldn't that be presupposed as a human being?

I've woken up early. I stare at the couch, at the place where I sat on February 22, and think about that evening. I think too much. That's why I'm not a good sleeper, especially when I'm away from home. It's dark inside the room. It's darker outside the room. Remote communities have a different kind of darkness. Up here, the sky is an endless black canvas, and you could spend your entire life counting the stars and never finish, and not want to. The stars are hypnotic in their brilliance. Up here, they and the moon are nature's streetlights. I lie in bed, curled up to fit, and look away from the couch, out the window at the soft white light. I listen to my heartbeat.

I don't like this hotel room. There are ghosts in here, memories I wish I didn't have. It's the one place in Norway House I'd prefer not to see again. I want to leave this room. I want to have new memories. I want to be with Dad. I check the time. We're supposed to meet in the lobby in half an hour. I wait out the thirty minutes by shifting onto my back and turning my attention to the blank white ceiling. I play images on it as though it's a movie screen. I imagine all the yesterdays that brought us to today, and I think about what's in front of us. For now, it's enough to get me through.

IT'S APPROPRIATE THAT in 1955, when twenty-year-old Donald Robertson left the community for Cook Christian Training School, thousands of miles away in Phoenix, Arizona, it was on the water. When Dad left Norway House before freeze-up and headed out onto the trapline with his family, he did so in a canoe, on the rivers and lakes, framed by the diverse population of trees that lined the shores. When he left for the trapline with his father each spring, forgoing the last months of school in favour of the muskrat run, it was in the same way. I would think the familiarity of the river helped ease him into the challenges a new and bigger world would present.

The boat that took people to Selkirk, the SS *Keenora*, was too large to travel on the Nelson River, so the first part of Dad's journey was a short one—less than twenty miles on a smaller steamboat from Norway House to Big Mossy Point, near Warren Landing. From there, after having lunch on the shore, he transferred onto the SS *Keenora*, which travelled a regular route from

Winnipeg to the northern end of Lake Winnipeg from 1923 until it was decommissioned in 1966. Dad was on the large steamboat for a few days, cruising across Lake Winnipeg, each moment taking him farther and farther away from home, until he docked in Selkirk, Manitoba, northeast of Winnipeg.

Keith, the man who was supposed to pick Dad up in the town, wasn't there; either the boat had arrived early or Keith was late. For a time, Dad was alone in a strange place. It can't be overstated just how alien and hard an urban setting is for those used to living in a remote community. And this isn't exclusive to a specific time period. There are more transitional supports available to people coming from a place like Norway House today than there were sixty-five years ago, but still, the shift is jarring.

I saw this first-hand in the program I ran preparing Indigenous People from community to enter the manufacturing industry in the city. I realized very early on that the preparation had to be not only skills-based but also transition-based. An Indigenous person coming to an urban location for the first time faces many of the same challenges an immigrant faces: racism, poverty, language barriers, among others. And there are more practical challenges. For example, as much as an individual in my program needed to be taught how to work with machinery, she also needed to be taught how to use the transit system—how to get a bus pass, how to transfer from one bus to another. If the person lacked that type of support, the culture shock alone could be enough to send her back to the familiarity and safety of home. And who would blame her?

Dad experienced culture shock as soon as he stepped off the SS *Keenora*. In Keith's absence, he decided to walk downtown, killing time until his friend showed up to take him into Winnipeg.

His introduction to Selkirk was the first in a series of new experiences, each one more difficult than the last: Selkirk, then Winnipeg, then Phoenix.

There were many things Dad saw for the first time in wandering through the streets of Selkirk that day. Like, well, streets. His feet walked atop unfamiliar surfaces—concrete sidewalks and asphalt roads, for people and automobiles, respectively. Speaking of automobiles, there was one government truck in his home community, but in Selkirk, there were cars everywhere he turned—as well as streetlights and traffic lights, which were also new to him. The streetlights cast a lazy orange glow onto the buildings that lined the sidewalks, shoulder to shoulder, with little space between. It must've been suffocating, and this feeling would have only been compounded when Keith finally showed up and took Dad into Winnipeg.

But Dad found himself able to adapt, to make the transition effectively. The time he'd spent with non-Indigenous people in Norway House had surely helped him gain confidence, as had knowing how to speak English fluently. But there was something less tangible at play. He credited his ability to adjust to the strength of the Cree people of Norway House; he believed that somehow he'd inherited an attribute or value that helped him. Because, he told me, they'd had to adjust from one way of life to another. From living on the land to following a more domesticated (as Dad once put it) way of life. From learning everything they needed to know on the land to learning in the classroom, at either the residential school or one of the many day schools in the area. From the traditional practices and ways of living that had been passed down from one generation to the next to the ubiquitous influence of Christianity. I can report that while the community has its struggles today, it has persevered. The Cree are a strong people, a proud people, and so, too, are my Indigenous brothers and sisters across Turtle Island.

Dad had survived those changes in the community, and now more changes were required—a reality that must have hit him strongly during that first walk through the streets of Selkirk and stayed with him when he boarded the bus to Phoenix from Winnipeg. With each mile that passed, as the bus moved relentlessly towards Arizona, the world changed a bit more, kept getting bigger, kept requiring Dad to grow with it. At times, he would succeed in acclimating himself with the same practicality that he'd carried with him his entire life. Other times, he would fall victim to inexperience, but after getting back onto his feet, he'd learn from those challenges.

Deep in the southern United States, somewhere in the state of Texas, after Dad finished eating lunch at a diner, he headed for the bathroom before climbing back onto the bus. He looked back and forth between the white bathroom and the black bathroom, wondering which one he should use. Segregation was unfamiliar to him; that one group of people could be set apart from another based solely on race just didn't make sense. But eventually, he settled on the black bathroom, reasoning to himself that he was much darker than white.

This was one of many new choices that presented themselves to Dad. Some were troubling to him—he couldn't believe you were designated to one place or another by the colour of your skin. Other decisions he had to make were, in hindsight, comical, but arguably no less overwhelming or confusing.

The bus stopped for meals at diners and truck stops. You'd eat, take a bathroom break, then get back on the bus. One of the later stops was at a buffet in New Mexico. There, Dad was faced with such a variety of foods that he'd never eaten or even seen before. It might've been a small comfort when he saw the price for the massive assembly line of dinner options. Too rich for his blood. So he ordered a hamburger instead. Two, in fact. The trip was almost over, and he wouldn't have money to eat again, so he decided to load up.

For several days, he'd eaten nothing but hamburgers. He liked hamburgers, and he loved ketchup. Dad went through the line, paid for his burgers, and found a booth where he could sit and enjoy a cheap and familiar meal. All these restaurants had bottles of ketchup at each table, ready to be used. A novelty. Dad slathered so much of the condiment onto his food that his plate looked like a crime scene. He opened wide and took a big bite, and that's when his mouth caught on fire. It wasn't ketchup on the table but hot sauce. The hottest you could get. He scraped off as much as he could from the remaining burgers, but a lot of hot sauce remained, and he had to finish them or go hungry.

By the end of August, Dad had arrived in Phoenix and started at Cook Christian Training School, an institution established in 1911 by Reverend Charles H. Cook to teach the Pima Indians in Sacaton. Affiliated with the Presbyterian Church, the school provided training to prepare Indigenous People for work within the church in their own communities. As far as Dad knows, he was the first Indigenous Canadian to attend Cook Christian, opening the door for others who followed. That year, there were sixteen Indigenous nations represented. Sixteen nations, sixteen dialects—none of which were Cree. While this widened the gap between Dad and his home community—a detachment that he may not have recognized at the time—it also served to further expand his world. It was interesting to meet so many different American Indians, to be exposed to their distinct cultures, to find out, through the friendships he made, how they were different and how they shared historical and contemporary experiences.

Soon after Dad arrived, the program changed from four years to three. Having committed to the original longer term, he decided that he would stay in Phoenix and spend the last year taking university courses and pursuing a mature student diploma. It may come as a surprise to all those whom Dad told he had only an eighth-grade education, but he wrote the GED and passed it in 1959. "I say that I have only an eighth-grade education," he told me, "to keep people off guard."

Dad learned a great deal about Christianity and leadership at Cook Christian, both in the classroom and through volunteer work in the local Black community, where he spent time with kids and attended services. This, too, proved to be interesting and enriching. Simply by sitting there and listening, he learned about their food, customs, ways of living, values. Sixty-five years later, this reflects the spirit of reconciliation that Dad and I share, which centres around the importance of listening. I wonder if his experience made the concept of black and white bathrooms even more baffling to him. I wonder if those who advocated for the use of segregated bathrooms might've changed their minds if they had just sat and listened. This might be simplifying a complex issue, but at times, simple solutions are incredibly hard to achieve. Getting two people to sit across from each other, to talk and listen to each other, and to do so without preconceptions is hard. But, I would argue, necessary.

DAD'S FIRST CHRISTMAS away from Norway House was also his first Christmas without snow. All the other students at Cook Christian went home for the holidays, but Dad did not. He couldn't afford to, and even if money hadn't been an issue, it was so far away. He'd get on a bus, make the days-long journey, and then have to turn around and come right back. At least he wasn't alone; a skeleton crew of staff members stayed behind, mostly maintenance workers, because they had to look after the facility. One of those who remained was named John Wilson. One day, outside the otherwise empty building, the two of them, left to their own devices, sat together. It was quiet and hot.

"What do you think, Don?" John asked.

"Well," Dad said, "it's sure not Christmas. Christmas has snow."

John's experience, for all Dad knew, was the opposite. Living in the Deep South, he might never have seen snow.

He shrugged. "When you think about it, this is what it was like in Palestine when Jesus was a baby."

Dad tilted his head thoughtfully and waited for John to continue.

"There was no snow!" his new friend explained. "Don, we're in the *real* Christian world now."

Dad looked around, at the dry earth, at the hot the sun, and nodded, "Yeah, I guess you're right!"

Phoenix was where Dad found his unconditional, undying love for basketball. Throughout a long and fulfilling life, he has had perhaps only two greater loves: Mom and his children. (Okay, maybe golf.) But basketball has been a staple in Dad's life, and he in turn has been a staple to basketball. In Winnipeg, he was known for attending almost every university basketball game for years: the University of Winnipeg Wesmen, the University of Manitoba Bisons, and the Brandon University Bobcats (a two-hour drive away). Even in the 1980s, when I didn't know Dad very well, I knew how much he loved basketball; it's why I took to the game in high school despite feeling the strong pull of hockey (as many kids do in Canada). In grade ten, I had to choose one or the other because doing both had become untenable. I chose basketball because of Dad.

Dad's infatuation with the sport may have been the result of boredom. Unromantic, maybe, but when he wasn't sitting around with John talking about the weather, he shot baskets. The students had made a small court so they could play together when they had downtime, and during the holidays, Dad would practice free throws, jump shots, layups, and dribbling. During his first year at the institution, he was awful, which was understandable. He'd never touched a basketball in his life. By the end of four years, though, he wasn't too bad. The basketball team he and his classmates started—the one with the team picture where Dad looks exactly like me—played in the YMCA league. While he didn't get quite good enough to help the team win any tournaments, they were awarded most sportsmanlike once.

DAD WENT BACK home to Norway House the first two summers between school years, but he didn't go onto the land. Instead, he picked up where he'd left off, doing what he and the family used to do over the summers when they weren't on the trapline: fishing. When he was younger, he would help his father; now he did it all himself. He bought and set his own nets, and sold what he caught to the fisheries at Warren Landing. This was one of the ways Dad made money for the return journey to Phoenix. The other sources of income were the two summer jobs he did when fishing was over. First, he worked with his brother Allan Ross, who was in charge of developing X-rays for the community. The next summer, he worked with Charlie Queskekapow, hauling sand from Rossville to where they were building a new hospital. Charlie had a barge, and Dad would load up the sand and make three or four trips a day across Little Playgreen Lake. On the way there, Dad would jump off the barge and swim, hanging on to the rope to get pulled through the water.

The last two summers, Dad worked as a student minister, first in Gods Lake Narrows, then in Gods River. He particularly enjoyed the time he spent in Gods Lake Narrows because that was the reserve where Nana was born and lived before moving to Norway House to attend residential school. While ministering to the community, he got to meet relatives for the first time. He would conduct sermons in the church and visit people anywhere else he could: in their homes, on the land. "In this way," Dad said, "I began to feel like a little Walter Keeper."

Nana went down to Phoenix, by boat and then by bus, when Dad graduated from Cook Christian Training School. It was the first time she'd left Norway House since arriving there as a young girl decades earlier. She would later travel all the way to British Columbia to watch Dad graduate from Union College on the UBC campus. Ibbs Avery had heard about how well Dad was doing in Phoenix and in the summers at Gods Lake and Gods River, and wanted him to do preaching missions for the United Church on Vancouver Island, then along the West Coast (at Bella Bella, Bella Coola, Hartley Bay, and other communities).

The preaching missions in British Columbia were so success-ful (an article about Dad's time there called him a fiery evangelist and likened his appearance to that of a football hero) that the United Church asked him to do another year-long mission, this time in Manitoba. He was to visit fourteen reserves, including Nelson House, South Indian Lake, Oxford House, Gods Lake Narrows, Red Sucker Lake, Garden Hill, Berens River, and Little Grand Rapids. The tour of these communities would end at home: Norway House Cree Nation.

This was where Dad found out just how much he had learned, and the weight of what he had lost. The last time he'd spoken Swampy Cree was after his third year in Phoenix, when he was a student minister in Gods Lake Narrows. And even then, language use was intermittent. He spoke Cree during those first three summers, but not in between. There were no other Cree speakers at Cook Christian, so he had nobody to speak it to.

There Dad was, minutes before the afternoon service, sitting in the front pew, waiting to give his first sermon on the last stop of his northern Manitoba mission. He could feel tension throughout his entire body, something he was unfamiliar with and may not have understood. I, on the other hand, know it all too well: anxiety. Something had changed. Certainly in him; maybe in the community. Had he left as one person and returned as somebody else? Would they accept him? His brother Allan was at his side.

"Do you think you could go up and say something in Cree first?" Dad asked.

"Of course," said Allan, who at one time served as Chief of the community.

He got up and addressed the large group of people packed inside that small church near the waterfront. He said that Dulas had asked him to speak first, and he talked for a long while. With each word in Swampy Cree rolling off his tongue like poetry, a peace came over Dad. When the time came for him to deliver the sermon, he did so confidently. Allan had calmed his mind, as though he were back on the land, listening to the wind, embraced by the trees and the water. By this time, he'd been doing this for years. He was a fiery evangelist, according to that article. With four years of schooling under his belt, he knew God well and had been working to tell others about Him—in British Columbia, in the thirteen reserves he'd visited in Manitoba before coming to Norway House. He thought back to Gods Lake Narrows, to the summer he'd spent there. He was a little Walter Keeper. He could do this. And he did. He was certain that he was delivering the sermon of his life, and right there in the congregation, witnessing it, were his father, James, and his mother, Sarah. Nana looked overcome with emotion.

I can relate to what Dad must've been feeling, how hard he must've tried to give the best sermon he was capable of delivering because his parents were in the crowd. When I was in high school playing for the Kelvin Clippers and Dad was in the stands, it motivated me, gave me a burst of energy. His presence gave me the energy a Red Bull might give others. Even now, when Mom and Dad come to one of my readings or lectures, I try just a bit harder because I want to make them proud. I'm sure that all Dad wanted to do that Sunday afternoon was make his mother proud. I'm sure that he kept glancing over to meet her eyes and see how he was doing.

After the service, on the skiff on the way home from the church to Robertson Bay, slicing through the waters of Little Playgreen Lake, Dad sat with Nana. He turned towards her but couldn't read her face, couldn't tell what she was thinking, how she was feeling. Had he done as well as he thought?

"Mom, what's wrong? How did I do?" he asked.

She exhaled as though she'd been holding her breath since leaving the rocky shore by the church.

"Oh, Dulas," she said, "you almost made me cry."

Dad puffed out his chest, straightened his collar. A smile overtook his face.

"Why?" he asked. "Was I that good?" It was obvious to him. He'd done so well that he nearly brought his mother to tears.

"No," Nana said. "Your Cree was so bad."

All residential schools forbade children to speak their Indigenous languages because the government knew how important language is to culture. Language is not like riding a bike; if you don't use it, you will eventually lose it. In her time at Norway House Indian Residential School, Nana would've had to break the rules to speak Cree. I can guess—although it's only conjecture because Nana never told her story—that these restrictions had an adverse effect on her and her classmates. Elder Betty Ross shared her experience at Cross Lake Residential School with me. One day, she dared whisper in Cree to a friend of hers between classes, and this was overheard by a nun who'd been consistently horrendous to Betty. The nun shoved her against a wall, and when Betty fell to the ground, the nun kicked her in the head so hard that she lost hearing in one ear. Betty was no older than ten at the time, and she still wears a hearing aid because of this assault.

I'll never fully know how Nana was impacted by this act of cultural genocide, but I can say two things with certainty: first, she had an unshakeable belief in the role of education in surviving in an increasingly white world; and second, she placed immense importance on the value of knowing your own language. When she heard her son butcher the words he'd been raised to speak, the words that held all the knowledge he'd learned as a child on the trapline, it almost brought her to tears.

Nana knew the importance of language. She didn't want

Dad to lose it, but he was. In that moment, on the skiff heading back to Robertson Bay, Dad realized it. Before then, he only knew that he wasn't speaking Swampy Cree as gracefully, as naturally, as he had before. But over the years, starting with that first day of school and continuing on through the advanced education his mother so desperately wanted him to have, he began to lose the words.

From that moment forward, he endeavoured to relearn the language. When he read books in English, he translated them in his head into Swampy Cree, word by word, line by line, page by page. When he thought, he did so exclusively in Swampy Cree. And he spoke to others in Swampy Cree whenever he could. He was back home for the time being, on the last leg of his preaching mission, and there were people he could talk to in the language. The more he spoke, the more it came back to him. He found the words, and he knew that no matter where he went from there, he would take them with him. He would not lose them again.

ONCE DAD HAD finished his year-long mission in Manitoba, the United Church sent him to the West Coast. For six months, he replaced a counsellor at the residential school in Port Alberni on Vancouver Island. From there, he moved to the Friendship Centre in Prince Rupert, where he stayed for three years. Then he moved again, and again, and again, all along the coast of British Columbia, from Kispiox to Hazelton to another place and then another. Throughout, he continued to make the same kind of impression he'd made on his first visit to British Columbia: the fiery evangelist who looked like a football hero.

The travelling finally stopped when the United Church made arrangements for Dad to study theology at Union College on the University of British Columbia campus in Vancouver. The church was low on ministers, and in response, it had developed a shortened four-year program. (Normally the training took three years longer.) Dad took classes from autumn to spring, then worked as a student minister in the fishing village of Namu over the summer months, conducting services on Sundays, doing visitations during the week, and working at the cannery—dumping fish from their bins to the conveyor belts and hosing everything down afterwards, all the guts and blood—in order to make enough money to pay for school.

When he graduated as an ordained minister, he received a letter from the United Church advising him that he'd been assigned to a church on reserve. "An Indian should preach to Indians," the letter read, which did not sit well with Dad. Graduates had no say in what pastoral charge they were given, and that was fine, but he knew that white ministers weren't being assigned only to white communities. It wasn't equitable treatment, and Dad wouldn't have any of that. He wasn't an Indian minister; he was a minister. I've felt the same way in my writing career. I love being recognized as an Indigenous writer by my colleagues and by Indigenous kids who might be inspired by what I've accomplished, but someday I want to be known as a great writer, not as a great *Indigenous* writer, which seems to imply that the measures of excellence are different between the two. They aren't. Or at least, they shouldn't be.

Dad wrote back to the church to say that he wouldn't have minded the assignment if it had gone through regular channels, but it clearly had not. He'd received the same training as everybody else, and he should be given the same consideration. This was important to him. It was his right as a student who had taken the same courses, who had paid for his own education, who had graduated from the same program.

Not long after, the church responded with news of a different pastoral charge in a non-Indigenous community. To this day, Dad isn't sure if the assignment was punishment for sticking up for himself or simply the equal treatment he'd asked for. Whatever the reason, he was assigned to Melita, Manitoba, a town he'd never heard of.

KĒKACH-MITATAHT (NINE)

I pack up and leave the hotel room at last and find Dad waiting in the lobby, in the sinking couch, looking fresh and ready to go. This is more like him. Being late at the airport was an outlier. He's probably been up at least as long as me and doing more productive things than staring at a couch, out a window, or at the ceiling.

A cool breeze mouths at our skin when we leave the hotel, a breath coming in off Little Playgreen Lake. We're meeting our guide, Eric Ross, at the York Boat Diner for breakfast before heading out onto the land. We take a long time to make the short walk from the hotel to the restaurant because Dad moves slowly, but I don't mind the pace. The subtle wind follows us across the parking lot in whispers, but it'll be gone soon enough. I was worried about the weather leading up to the trip, but the sky is perfect.

Eric's waiting for us outside the restaurant, leaning against the front of his truck. He's probably in his sixties, with grey hair in a military brush cut, and he's thick. Stocky. Some people look like their dogs; Eric looks like his truck. But he's warm and friendly—I can see it instantly when the three of us exchange salutations. He talks to us like he's known us for years, not a few seconds. Most Norway House community members are like this. They have a small-town congeniality that I recall from my summers in Melita.

Inside the restaurant, Dad sees somebody he's known for years, Charlie's nephew Grant Queskekapow, another United Church minister. The server has just delivered his breakfast, and we join him at his table. The only English I hear for the next half hour is when we order our food—Dad a hard-boiled egg and me a bowl of oatmeal and some toast. Otherwise, Grant, Eric, and Dad speak in Swampy Cree. I don't understand any of it. I just sit there smiling broadly, laughing when the others laugh, as though I'm in on the joke. I love hearing Dad speak Cree, I always have, but there's something bittersweet about it, and the two opposing feelings can be hard to reconcile. I'm always brought back to that conversation we had driving home from the golf course in Winnipeg one afternoon, when he said his biggest regret was not teaching me his language.

I regret it as well, especially in moments like this. Not only because I feel left out, although that's a part of it, but because, after all the work I've done to establish a firm sense of who I am, of my indigeneity, it feels like there's a piece missing. I say *ekosani* when thanking people in public, in emails, in book inscriptions, on social media, but the word feels somehow empty. So I smile and I laugh and I listen, all the while wondering what could have been different, despite a promise I made to myself not to regret the past, because it's part of the journey that led me here.

Our meals arrive, and I'm thankful for full mouths and brief lulls in conversation, slight reprieves from my own insecurity. But even in that diffidence, I can't help but enjoy Dad's boyish excitement and energy, things I haven't seen all that much from him over the last several years. At one point, Grant breaks into English and asks what we're all doing in the community.

"We're going out to Black Water," Dad says, and he just sounds happy. There's no other way to describe it. "I haven't been there for a long time."

He draws out the word "long."

They say more to each other in Swampy Cree, then Dad slips into English again. They're talking about both traplines he's mentioned to me.

"—at the end of that there's another little lake, and that's where, what I can remember, that's where we went. The southern part of that lake, through a small river. And Black Water, I can remember little bits of it. I know there's a lake behind the trees, just a little behind the land, behind there somewhere. I used to walk over there."

Dad's told me these things before, about his time on the land. We remember things like this. The older we get, the more these pieces disconnect and the harder it becomes to relate them to each other. In the oral tradition, these memories would have been preserved in stories passed down from generation to generation. For years, Dad didn't have anybody to tell these stories to. He talks, now, in the language of lost memories. He talks in pieces that he tries to connect but cannot. I think about this in the silence that follows and hope that once we're at Black Water, these pieces connect and stay connected.

DAD WAS THIRTY-TWO years old and starting work as an ordained minister in August 1967. He came to a small town that felt at once alien and familiar to him. Melita shared similarities with Rossville; the relative isolation made for a strong sense of community more easily obtained than in larger urban centres. Everybody knew everybody else, and when a stranger came to town, people were aware. I'm sure all the citizens of Melita knew of Dad's arrival. They had never had a young minister before, let alone a Cree minister. There must have been a swell of curiosity and interest. The United Church had wanted the Indian minister to preach to Indians, but Melita was a sea of white faces.

This is not the story of racism and discrimination you might expect, however, given the circumstances: a Cree minister arrives in an all-white farming town. I mean, how could it *not* be that kind of story? Didn't it usually go the other way? Didn't the whites preach to the Indians? Dad should've been run out of town! He swears on the Bible, though, that he never once encountered racism during all the years he lived and worked in Melita.

"I'M NOT AN elephant," Dad once told a room full of non-Indigenous special education workers. They were offering support to students in First Nations communities throughout Manitoba. "I'm not an elephant, and neither are you."

What does that even mean? I've heard the idiom "the elephant in the room" countless times. It means there's something pressing that nobody wants to talk about. But how does it apply to Dad avoiding racism despite being an Indigenous person in a white town? As he tells it, if he had arrived in Melita under the watchful eye of the townsfolk and announced to them that he was Cree, that would have been akin to saying, "I am an elephant." He would have been telling them that they should pay attention to him not because he's a minister but because he's Cree.

Still, it wasn't as though he was hiding from his identity. Before coming to Melita, he'd chaperoned a dozen UBC students who were in a musical, performing shows all the way across Canada on their way to Expo 67 in Montreal. They had stopped in Portage La Prairie, and people from Melita came down to, in Dad's words, check him out. They knew he was Cree already, so he didn't see the point of shining a spotlight on it. Doing so might have created expectations based on stereotypes that were rampant at the time. Not just in small-town Melita, but everywhere. Like at a junior high school in Winnipeg.

When I was a teenager, I was often able to take advantage of the fact that I didn't look, sound, or act like the "Indian" people thought they knew. With my trained eye today, I can look back at my school picture and see that I looked Cree, but kids back then, and very likely people in Melita, had received a different sort of training—the racist stereotypes prevalent in popular culture. The burnt-toast incident happened because that boy had noticed my dark skin, not because he thought I was Indigenous; I made that connection myself later. Dad's always had short hair, that military-style brush cut, and in my memory, he frequently wore a suit. I have a photo of him walking down a city sidewalk, and he looks like he's from Wall Street. Where were the braids? Where were the moccasins? The buckskin jacket?

The elephant Dad was referring to was the stereotype and how it clouds our interactions. If we present ourselves as one thing—say, an Indigenous minister—it can perpetuate stereotypes and force us to meet each other as those stereotypes. Dad was interested in people connecting as human beings, not as an Indian and a white person. That's how he approached life, and as much as he respected who he was and where he'd come from, he wasn't going to Melita as an Indigenous person—he was going as a minister. This didn't make him *not* an Indigenous person, but it may have introduced townspeople to a different idea of what an Indigenous person was.

DAD MADE A point to extend his presence beyond the church, and he became heavily involved in the community. He had a unique approach to the role of a minister, in that his aim was not to convert people away from who they were, as others had advocated, but to introduce Christianity in a way that enriched lives and brought people together. It wasn't about creating a gap; it was about bridging it.

"You had to live their life in order to understand their life."

I can't help but think this philosophy was informed heavily by Dad's first experiences in school. This was what he wrote about almost twenty-five years later in his "Speaking in Tongues" essay. The untanned woman who stood in front of the Cree children in that one-room schoolhouse may have lived in the community, but she didn't live the life, and as a consequence, she didn't understand the life. This made her connection to the students and the community tenuous. The learning environment suffered, and the students struggled.

Dad, on the other hand, immersed himself in small-town life.

While serving in Melita, he became president of the Kinsmen Club. He described it to me as a service cult (surprise, Dad was in a cult!), but the Kinsmen Club was founded in 1920 with the goal of working to better communities across Canada. Enhance well-being, improve the environment. In Melita, the most significant thing the Kinsmen did was build the swimming pool. *That* swimming pool.

For obvious reasons, I'd have been just as happy if there were no pool at all, but I won't revisit past traumas again. It does serve, however, as a stark reminder of what I encountered in the town, and how surprising it is that Dad had no interactions like it. Of course, I was not in a position of authority, while Dad was. Ministers carry an air of authority, do they not? They command respect. A brown kid in a blizzard of white faces doesn't. Many people knew me in Melita, mostly because of who my grandparents were, but I never lived there, was never as active in the town as Dad. I was never seen as a community member. Dad most certainly was.

People who studied theology at Union College were required to pick a specialty. Dad chose to specialize in counselling because it was something he'd always felt drawn to. From first-hand experience, I can see why. He's good at it. Dad's always my dad, but from time to time, he's also my counsellor. I often consider myself fortunate that I have my psychiatrist and my father.

Dad did quite a bit of counselling in Melita, in particular with young people. They responded to him because he was good at what he did, but he thinks his age had something to do with it, too, and I wouldn't disagree. He was a young minister, probably more relatable. It's like the deacon and the teachers in Norway House who connected strongly with the youth there. Dad got to know the young people in Melita through counselling and the

Kinsmen Club, and by starting a fastball team that did well immediately and even won tournaments.

Dad started the town's first basketball team too. A girls' team, formed from a group of kids who'd never played before. He said that he almost had to present them with a ball and say, "This is a ball." But like the kids on the fastball team, the girls were athletes, so they took that ball and started to dribble, then pass, then shoot. The first year, they played only exhibition games, but in their second year, partially because there weren't many good rural teams (as much as I think Dad was probably a serviceable coach, this wasn't a *Hoosiers* situation), they won games in league play. By the time he left Melita, the team had been to the district finals.

There were popular sports before Dad arrived in the community. He bowled and curled, the latter as a spare for Grandpa Eyers's team. Both were sports he'd not played before, and in the summer he tried another sport that he would eventually fall in love with: golf. In Melita, though, his time on the links was perhaps more significant because my maternal grandpa taught him how to play.

"I thought it was a silly game at first," Dad said. "You hit a ball and chase it across a lawn? That's it?" Suffice to say, he didn't get the bug for it until after he left Melita, but on the course, he strengthened a friendship that he'd already been developing with my grandpa. Maxwell Eyers held a number of positions in the community, and he and my grandmother Kathleen were prominent citizens. They owned a furniture store on Main Street and a warehouse on Front Street, and Grandpa was also the ambulance driver, a prize-winning gardener, and the undertaker (when I was a kid, according to my mother, I saw Grandpa's embalming machine and asked him if I could have a milkshake). Because of his work with the departed, he and Dad spent a great deal of time with each other. Whenever Dad had a funeral service to do, he'd work with my grandpa, and because Dad was also responsible for two nearby communities, Napinka and Tilston, they would often travel together.

"We became good friends," Dad said, then he paused and chuckled. "When I stole his daughter, that changed a little bit."

MOM. BEVERLY EYERS. When Dad first came to Melita, she was living in Winnipeg, working as a social worker, and wasn't around all that often. But she came home one weekend and attended Dad's service, and when he saw her in the congregation, it took his breath away. (I'm putting words into his mouth, but judging by the way Dad talks about Mom, it's entirely plausible that he had a visceral response like this when seeing her for the first time.) He was still breathless when he saw her face to face after the service—so much so that he couldn't get one word out.

"I was shy," Dad explained. "I didn't have a lot of confidence back then, especially with a beautiful girl like that. I mean, why would she want to see me?"

Considering how engaged Dad was with the town and the other communities he'd worked in, it's interesting to hear that he was shy and self-doubting, but I can relate to this. A lot of writers can. A lot of people can. It's like Dad said: we're all human beings. I've been lucky enough to meet many great writers, and I have found that even some of the best have imposter syndrome. Even the best can be shy in the hospitality suite at a festival. I'm not even close to the best, but I've worked hard to overcome my anxiety, my shyness, my low self-esteem, to go to the hospitality suite and meet other writers, try to act like I'm not a gargantuan ball of nerves asking myself why anybody would want to talk to me. I suppose Dad found a way, in interacting with communities, in embedding himself within the social fabric of them, to overcome his own shyness and lack of confidence. Even when it came to finding the words to talk to a beautiful girl. Lucky for me he did.

The businessmen and older people in Melita had a place where they would go for coffee on Saturdays, and Dad would walk down from the church to join them. One Saturday, a week after he'd seen Mom for the first time and had failed to utter a syllable to her, Dad crossed Ash Street and made his way towards the coffee shop. That's when he saw her again, working on Grandpa's car with my grandparents' dog, Juby, yapping at her feet.

Dad had a wry smile on his face when he told me that Mom was working on the car. Mom has two university degrees, raised three boys on her own, and is a very capable human being, but she's not handy like that. I've never once seen her perform vehicle maintenance. She denies this incident ever happened, while Dad swears that it was a trap, that she used the car as a way to lure him in. I'm not sure who to believe, but there's one fact they agree on, and it's the only fact that matters: he asked her to join him for coffee, and she said yes.

They walked to the coffee shop together, found a table, and sat across from each other, steam billowing from their cups, under the scrutiny of the old people and businessmen. One of those old people, Billy Clark, even sat with them as a sort of chaperone. His presence, and frankly, the presence of all the old people and businessmen, prevented this coffee date, and others that followed, from being an *actual* date. Their first real date, as it turned out, was in the city. The Russian junior hockey team was

playing Team Canada at the Barn—the old Winnipeg Arena—
and Dad had made enough money to take a bus down to watch
the game. He invited Mom to join him, and the rest, as they say,
is history.

At some point in those early years, Mom switched jobs and
travelled to Montreal to train to be an airline stewardess. The
training lasted a few weeks, and for the first time since they'd
started dating, she and Dad were apart. When she was finished,
Mom worked as a summer replacement and flew all around the
country for Air Canada. She loved flying, but her schedule was
erratic. The rare times she was home in Winnipeg, Dad would
go and see her. At the end of the summer, Air Canada called her
to Toronto for a permanent position, but she decided to decline
the job offer. Soon after, my parents got engaged. Unfortunately, there's no story about a romantic proposal. "I'm not
good at those things," Dad said. "I'm not very romantic. When
we really started talking about it, Mom told me that I'd have to
ask her dad."

I don't know. I think there's something old-school romantic in asking a father for his daughter's hand in marriage. That's
what I did before proposing to Jill, and I'm not the most romantic human being either. I guess even a blind squirrel can find a
nut. And Grandpa must have thought carefully before offering
his approval. He must have had some consternation about their
marriage. What sort of difficulties would they face? What barriers
would they encounter? I don't want to make something out of
nothing, but the reality is, in the late 1960s, in a rural area like
Melita, interracial marriages were not common.

Time passed slowly in Melita, another similarity to Norway
House. It doesn't work the way it does in the city; it's viewed and
treated differently. And the way time passes brings a sort of peace

and calm to every movement, every moment. I have memories of that calm, just like Dad. It's sitting on the hood of Grandpa's truck in the middle of the night, staring up at the sky, before Shayne starts to play the Nitty Gritty Dirt Band. It's standing on the seventh tee of Melita Golf and Country Club, the bench dedicated to my grandfather's memory close by. I'm ready to track my ball through the air with nobody else around, with the lush green of the newly irrigated fairway in front of me. It's entering the bakery and breathing in deeply to catch the unmistakable scent of fresh buns. And for my dad, it's walking to the coffee shop on a quiet weekend morning and coming across a young woman working on a car.

Given how far Dad had travelled from home—to the southern United States, the western edge of Canada, Expo 67 in Montreal, and many places in between—it must have been comforting to be in a quiet place like that.

THE 1970S WERE another matter. As newlyweds, Mom and Dad lived apart because of their jobs, but she moved closer to Melita when she started a one-year teacher training program at Brandon University in the fall of 1970. They visited each other regularly, and Dad found a way to be with Mom more often when he signed up for a three-week course at Brandon General Hospital, part of a program to train ministers to become therapeutic counsellors.

Mom finished her teaching certificate in 1971, and after four years in Melita, it was time for Dad to move on as well. Almost two decades had passed since he left Norway House, and things were about to come full circle. The community had openings for a teacher at the school and a minister at the church. Dad had fancied himself a little Walter Keeper, and now he could be ministering right where Walter used to. And no doubt he felt the pull of the land and the water.

My parents had to interview for their prospective positions, but that felt perfunctory; Mom had a degree and a year's worth of training in education. Getting qualified teachers to work, and stay, in remote communities was difficult. It's still difficult. In large part, this has to do with the fact that they're paid less on reserve despite having to do, arguably, more challenging work. Generally, schools on reserve receive less funding per student than schools in rural and urban centres. Why? If the aim is to provide access to quality education, a treaty promise, then why create environments where good teachers, support workers, and specialists leave because their salaries aren't commensurate with the difficult jobs they have? Suffice to say, there was Mom, ready to work in Norway House, and within half an hour, she knew she had the position.

Dad—an ordained minister with a wealth of experience who had been raised in the community—was even better qualified for his position. It should have been simple. But his interviewers were all non-Indigenous, and none were from Norway House. They didn't live in or understand the lives of people from the community. The interview went all day long, and while there must have been intelligent job-related questions, some were insulting.

"Do you know how to paddle a canoe?" one interviewer asked.

One of the main stereotypes in literature and film is the dead Indian, an Indigenous person whose culture is a relic of the past. The interviewers would've known that Dad was Cree, they would've known that he was from Norway House Cree Nation, they would've known that he grew up on the land and the swift waters around it, but one still asked whether he knew how to paddle a canoe. If not a racist question, it was at best ignorant. It reminds me of the experiment proposed in Wasagamack in the 1930s, when the Indian agent wanted to try land-based education but with non-Indigenous teachers rather than community members and Elders who had spent their lives on the land.

I don't know how Dad responded to the paddling question. He couldn't remember. He waited to hear from the interview committee for as long as he could, days upon days, before accepting a position in Russell, Manitoba, a town in the westernmost part of the province, just off the Yellowhead Highway. As quickly as the chance for him to work back home had come, the moment passed. And as much as Dad talks about leaving the past where it is, I find myself thinking about this from time to time and asking, "What if?" Especially when I'm in Norway House.

I drive through the community, I walk through the old cemetery to visit my relatives, I fish on the water by Dad's trapline, I visit the Fort and stroll out onto the slanted boardwalk, I look out over Little Playgreen Lake, I sit down at Auntie Flora's rickety folding card table and watch another game of Crazy Eights between her and Uncle Oliver, I wave to people I've never met like they're old friends.

I wonder what my life would've been like if things had gone differently, if Dad had waited one more day and heard back from the all-white interview committee in Dauphin. "He can preach and paddle a canoe! Perfect for impromptu shoreline sermons, just like Jesus! Sold!" The last time I went to Norway House, a fourteen-year-old kid took me out onto the river to fish and was just as capable on the land as his grandfather. When I was

his age, I was playing Nintendo, watching Saturday morning car-
toons, trying to learn how to skateboard so I could fit in with
the cool kids. That kid was a man in the eyes of his people. If I'd
grown up in Norway House, my journey would've been different;
I would've been so very Cree. But then, as quickly as that thought
comes, there's another question: "What *is* being Cree?" If my
journey had been different, would I be who I am today? Would I
be better? Worse? Dad's life and my life have led and are leading
to something, somewhere, someone.

As it happened, Dad ended up as the United Church minister
in Russell, and Mom took a teaching job in Roblin, just thirty-
five minutes away. Their tenures there would be short-lived. By
the time my brother Cameron was born on September 5, 1972,
Dad had agreed to take a position at Brandon University. As soon
as Mom was well enough, following Cam's birth, they packed
their bags and moved. It was late September by then. Dad started
work as the counsellor/coordinator of the Indian-Métis Project
for Action in Careers through Teacher Education (IMPACTE), a
program promoting Indigenous education.

IT WAS A vital time in Canada for Indigenous People, particularly in the field of education. In 1969, the Trudeau government
had introduced the White Paper, another attempt to solve the
so-called Indian Problem (a puzzle that has yet to be cracked—
we Natives are like the Millennium Prize Problems). The White
Paper proposed abolishing legal documents like the Indian Act
and all the treaties. Indian status would be eliminated, and First
Nations People would become the responsibility of provincial
governments. Reserves would be subject to private property laws.
All special programs and considerations would be terminated.

The Department of Indian Affairs would be dissolved. The government's stated intention was equality—the idea was to eliminate laws and programs that applied to Indigenous Canadians but no one else—but the proposal was unsurprisingly met with shock and staunch opposition. The White Paper was an appropriate title; it read more like a policy of assimilation than equality, and it addressed none of the concerns raised by leaders across Turtle Island.

The White Paper was shelved in 1970, just as Indigenous organizations began to create their own documents in response to it. The Red Paper. The Brown Paper. And a 1971 position paper by the Manitoba Indian Brotherhood entitled *Wahbung: Our Tomorrows*, which outlined what Chiefs in the province wanted in the areas of economic and community development, health, and education. In the latter, for example, the *Wahbung* paper made a number of recommendations that would have reversed the historical and continued failings of government-run schools in Indigenous communities. At the time the paper was written, according to Verna Kirkness, an icon in the field of Indigenous education, approximately 90 percent of Indigenous students weren't graduating from grade twelve. I would argue that this deplorable dropout rate was due to some of the problems that Dad had identified long ago: the untanned teacher standing in front of Cree students and teaching to them from the unknown. Now extrapolate that into teachers, principals, and administrators running schools in Indigenous communities across Canada without knowledge or appreciation of traditional ways of living and knowing, without consideration of cultures and languages, without any foundation on which to build success for Indigenous children. It was a colonial system and would no longer be acceptable.

Indigenous People had a clear vision of how they wanted the future to look, and they wanted control of their schools. They wanted the future of their children in their hands, not the hands of the government. One of the recommendations in *Wahbung* was to transfer educational control to the local responsibility centre (the reserve). This became known as local control, and even though the Canadian government predictably ignored *Wahbung*, it had a significant impact for Indigenous People, including Dad. Local control was a guiding force in his approach to Indigenous education, one of the central tenets of his philosophy.

In the early 1980s, Dad wrote an article about the growing awareness among Indigenous People that success for their children meant taking responsibility for their education. That building self-image and confidence in young people involved presenting their cultures in a positive way, not as something that needed to be eliminated or didn't hold intrinsic value. That doing so would improve motivation, learning, and self-worth. In the article, he discussed at length local control, parental involvement, and the need to integrate cultural content in the curriculum. "Often, when native culture is discussed in the classroom, there is a feeling that sub-standards are creeping in," he wrote. "In other words, doing things differently is equated with lowering standards. As native educators, we believe curriculum relevance can be achieved without lowering academic standards. Native studies must not be equated with low standards. Rather, it must be understood as striving for relevance and equality in all levels of academic achievement."

It's astonishing to consider that while Dad's article was written in the early 1980s, there has been significant movement in these areas only in the past ten years. Dad was a trailblazer, but even decades ago, these concepts weren't revolutionary; in hindsight, they seem fundamental, necessary, given the history of this country and its treatment of Indigenous People. Of course Indigenous People should have control over their own systems in their own communities, including their schools.

The residential school system and the trauma borne by survivors have been passed down from one generation to the next. Fear and distrust of schools can be undone only by involving parents in their children's learning experience, to build trust and, in so doing, improve success and educational attainment. Without question, Indigenous cultures and languages should be the foundation on which the curriculum is built.

Dad knew parents were needed. He knew Elders—grandparents who had knowledge and experience of a history that has not been written, of languages and values, of the known of Indigenous cultures—were needed. He knew Native educators were needed, people who could stand in front of a classroom of Indigenous students and present the known of their world before leading them into the unknown, as it always should have been.

AS THE DIRECTOR of IMPACTE, Dad came to know people in government, which proved to be important for his work. Federal funding was earmarked for programming to develop teaching jobs in the North. Dad and his colleagues at IMPACTE wanted to set up a training program so schools in Indigenous communities would have Indigenous teachers on staff. But somebody had to build the program, and there was no model on which to base it. Nothing like this had ever been done before.

It fell to Dad and his colleague Jack Loughton to do the heavy lifting. They created Brandon University Northern

Teachers Education Program (BUNTEP). It started off with two locations that used to be IMPACTE centres, in Camperville and The Pas (the first coordinator they hired was Strini Reddy, who would become a lifelong friend of Dad's), and grew rapidly. Soon, more centres opened in Nelson House, Island Lake, and Cross Lake.

BUNTEP was community-based. Local committees consisting of parents, representatives from Chief and Council, Elders, and teachers (both classroom educators and local people who knew land-based education) looked after the centres. *Their* centres, running *their* programs. It was what *Wahbung* had recommended and what Dad had wanted to see happen for so long.

He and his team worked tirelessly and relentlessly to build the program and make it a success. There was a lot of travelling in small planes, often in dangerous conditions. On a trip back to Brandon from one of the centres, Dad was travelling with Jack and Ovide Mercredi, former National Chief of the Assembly of First Nations. It's no secret that Dad used to be a bigger guy, and there was too much weight between the three men to use one aircraft, so they went in two: Dad in one, Jack and Ovide in the other. Dad's plane took off with no trouble, but the other plane went through the ice before takeoff. Thankfully, nobody was hurt.

There weren't many hotels in the communities. The best place to sleep, sometimes the only place, was on the floor of the school's staffroom. In anticipation of these arrangements, Dad and Jack used to travel with two bags each—one for clothing and the other for a sleeping bag. And more than once, Dad put socks on his hands because he'd forgotten mitts and had to push through long walks in the bitter northern cold to make meetings on time.

These sacrifices were worth it for what was accomplished, though, and the program's rapid growth was never at the expense of its quality or effectiveness. BUNTEP is still running today, only now it's called Kenanow and runs out of the University College of the North (an institution that Dad was involved in implementing). The nomination for Dad's honorary doctorate from Brandon University in 1992 said of his work on IMPACTE and BUNTEP: "He has placed Brandon University among the most creative institutions of higher education in Canada. The models he developed have been adapted for use in several other provinces and countries."

These sacrifices, while worth it, took their toll. Dad was getting worn out, and he needed a break from the program, especially with two young kids and a third on the way. During his tenure as director of BUNTEP, he'd taken a six-week counselling course at Brandon General Hospital (a continuation of the three-week course he'd completed when he and Mom were first married), and now there was a one-year program at the Pastoral Institute of Calgary. He was given a sabbatical from the university, and he, Mom, and their three boys (including newborn me) sold the house in Brandon and moved into a rented house in Calgary from the summer of 1977 until the summer of 1978.

When we came back to Brandon, things had changed. There was a new president at the university, and Dad wasn't the director of BUNTEP any longer. Instead, he was the coordinator of IMPACTE and BUNTEP. He didn't agree with the change, but he also felt that he'd taken both programs as far as he could, so he began to look for something else.

In 1979, he was offered the position of superintendent of the Manitoba Indian Education Board, a job that required him to make one last move after a lifetime of moves—this time to

Winnipeg. And so, Dad and his young family ended up on Queenston Street, in the neighbourhood of River Heights.

He continued to work and travel and spent less time at home. Mom became tired. It felt like she was raising three young boys on her own, and it was too much. She was angry at Dad for not being around, for leaving her with work that was as important as his. Dad, meanwhile, was resentful that she was angry. When Mom told him, soon after moving to Winnipeg, that she didn't want him around since he wasn't around anyway, he didn't think he deserved it.

My parents were both hurt, and Dad was gone. The loss to me, and I'm sure to my brothers, was immeasurable. Dad was a dream I had once, leaving shards of memories behind—memories that were replaced by fleeting moments, and even in those moments, in those most stubborn memories, he's leaving. Driving away from the house without me. Cam and Mike are in his car, smiling and excited for *Return of the Jedi*. I'm at the living room window, staring longingly, achingly through it. My breath is hot against the glass, fogging the window as though to prevent me seeing him leave. Why wasn't I old enough? Why wasn't he there? I knew I wouldn't see him for a week. To a little kid, a week is an eternity. I didn't know it then, but I know it now: a part of me was broken. I didn't know it then because Mom was there to hold the pieces of me together.

MITATAHT (TEN)

There's a gas station across the street from the mall. We make a quick stop before leaving the community for the trapline. I buy some snacks for the day, the healthiest stuff I can find, a large bottle of water, and at Eric's request, a margarine container full of frozen minnows.

We head out onto the road, Dad in the passenger seat of Eric's truck and me in the back. Eric and Dad speak Cree to each other the entire ride, and I feel serenaded by it while I watch the community give way to forest. Soon, there's nothing ahead of us but trees and the highway snaking fluidly through the wilderness like a stone river. It's paved from here until the ferry, but that's happened only within the last several years. Before that, it was mud and gravel, and you were at the mercy of the weather and resultant road conditions. If it was raining, a half-hour trip would, to the inexperienced and truck-less, take two or three times longer.

We follow unhurried turns and long straightaways where the road seems crushed by the forest on the horizon. Eric drives slowly, as though beholden to the relaxed pace, and I don't mind. While he and Dad continue to chat with each other, I study the scenery as it presents itself, then falls away. I try to notice the little things as we inch closer towards the end of the highway, where road meets river, where the ferry brings cars across the water until winter provides travellers with an ice road.

The grass blurs into a smear of vibrant green, as though we're travelling at warp speed, not twenty kilometres below the speed limit. My eyes train upwards and the trees move slowly across my line of sight, patiently beautiful. I focus on the calm, and it helps me, in turn, feel calm. Taking an anxiety pill, as I've done for the last several days, doesn't feel necessary today. In fact, I don't think of the tiny white pills at all. My breathing is deep and rhythmic; normally I have to recite "In for five seconds, out for seven seconds" in my head repeatedly to even it out. Free from those burdens, I focus on the unbroken string of trees and the long grass rising up against the trunks like flames, and let it wash over me as though pulling smoke across my body from a smudge bowl.

SINCE HIGH SCHOOL, I've believed that Mom and Dad raised me and my brothers to be non-Indigenous to protect us from the difficulties they knew we'd have growing up as Indigenous kids. That's why we moved to River Heights, that's why we went to the schools we did, that's why I was never told that I was

Indigenous—so I could avoid it, hide from it. That's why we were never taught Swampy Cree. If we knew the language, we'd know who we were; we'd be that much closer to our Indigenous identities. To make matters worse, Dad had read, and was even told, that if you knew two languages, you were going to fall behind. He believed it. If learning Swampy Cree was going to be detrimental to our cognitive development, he didn't want that. He didn't want us to be worse off than other kids. By the time he realized this was bullshit (he used the word "hogwash"), that having two languages is better than one, he figured it was too late. We'd started to grow up and were too old to teach.

Over the years, I've had to come to terms with the fact that I was raised this way, and find forgiveness for, or understanding of, my parents' decision to raise us non-Indigenous, to ensure we were closely associated with Mom's side of the family, and to keep us away from relatives on Dad's side so we wouldn't be exposed to the Cree part of who we were. I've had to come to terms with the fact that despite my parents' efforts to make me feel whole and connected, I always felt broken. I was Shel Silverstein's *The Missing Piece*, a book Mom read to me when I was a kid.

Later, I decided that this feeling was blood memory; no matter how much I was steered one way, the fabric of my being was steering me in the other direction. And oh, how much different my life would've been, the places I would've gone, if Mom and Dad had just told me who I was when I was a kid. How much easier this journey would have been.

One night when I was nineteen years old, Mom came into my bedroom. I was reading a comic. She sat down beside me, put her hand on my hand. Her fingers were cold, like icicles, like the life had been drained from her body. She told me that her father, my grandpa, had ALS. It sounds ridiculous and dramatic, but I used to imagine this was also how Mom and Dad might've told me that I was part Cree. They'd find me in my bedroom, sit me down, prepare me for the shock.

"David," they'd say. Sombre, serious. "You're Cree."

And then we'd deal with it. Deal with the fact that I was Native in a world that wanted Natives *not* to be Natives. What would my interactions have been like if I'd been aware of my identity at a young age? If I'd been taught what it meant to be Indigenous? Wouldn't I have been better equipped to deal with that red-headed kid? Ironically, he was actually the redskin, albeit from the blistering heat of the banana belt sun. Red-skinned and red-haired, chasing me around the Melita pool, calling me burnt toast. Wouldn't I have been able to tell the girl at my locker in grade eight, "Yeah, I'm an Indian. And it's not a tan—it's genetics. No tanning bed could ever get your skin to look like mine, sister. Sorry"? Wouldn't I have been able to see Vince at the party in the townhouse, perilously outside my River Heights comfort zone, and not think he was there to beat the shit out of me just because he was Native? Because hey, so was I. We might've hung out together, become friends; maybe he'd have become a mentor to me, since Dad was away. And what would Dad and I have talked about, that night after the party, when I told him he hadn't been a good father? Would I have wanted to talk to him at all? What would there have been for me to ask? What would there have been for him to say?

In all the speeches I've given since becoming a published writer, I've told the story of my life when I was without Dad, and later, when I was with him, after he and Mom got back together. This has been my truth. It has shaped who I am. It has helped to set the direction of my work. I have paid the dues of my identity to get where I am: a proud human being who is Cree, Scottish, Irish, and English.

But I've also been wrong.

"Me not learning about the Cree part of who I am, was that something intentional, or what guided that decision?" I asked Dad in 2019, in my office at work, him on the grey couch I'd bought from IKEA, me on an office chair, leaning forward as though watching an intense scene in a movie. I'd asked him thousands of questions over almost thirty years, but this was one I'd not asked. I can't explain why; I guess I'd just assumed the answer.

"You are who you are," he said. "We talked about Melita. I never went around telling people I was an Aboriginal person. People knew. I've never hidden the fact that's who I am, but it also doesn't do me any good walking around and saying, 'I want you to know that I'm an Aboriginal.' That's how I live. There's a way of life in being an Aboriginal that helps you be the person you are. One of the teachings of the Cree people is the concept of non-interference. That is, you don't interfere with another person's life. They're going to learn what they're going to learn. Since I am an Aboriginal, there's a part of me that still remembers that. That is, you don't interfere with another's life. You live the way you live, and by the way you live, that should show the kind of person you are. There was never an attempt for me to show you how to be an Aboriginal. I was going to teach you to be a man. In being a man, you're going to find out who you are, and you'll decide for yourself. I'm not going to decide for you who you are. It should show in my life, that within you there's a Cree stream, because I live that. But for me to have said, 'I'm going to teach you to be an Aboriginal'—how am I going to do that? How am I going to say, 'Well, now I'm going to teach you to be an Aboriginal person'? You are. I don't ever remember saying, 'This is the way I want you to live because you're an Aboriginal person.' I've tried to live a life that shows I am an Aboriginal person, and shows you that as well."

The choice my parents made, then, was not to hide the Indigenous part of our identity, our genetic makeup, or to raise us as non-Indigenous, but rather to raise us as humans and let us define for ourselves what it means to be Indigenous. Let us go on that journey of discovery in our own way, in our own time. And that begs the question: What is Indigenous identity?

How would Dad have taught me to be an Indigenous person? Taught me to be Cree? I *am* Cree. When he told me this, it made sense. I am Cree, I have always been Cree, and I will always be Cree. Being Cree meant something different when I was in junior high because I lacked the knowledge and had had only limited exposure to other Cree people, including Dad. I associated Cree with negativity. But I was still Cree. As I've grown older, my identity as a Cree man has grown with me, changed with me, evolved with me. Identity is fluid and personal. That's what I want you to keep in mind. This is my story. This is my identity. It is nobody else's. My truths are my own, and I've found out recently that some of the things I took to be truths were wrong. That's part of the journey too.

On the other hand, I wish he had given me *something*. I mean, I get it—he wanted me to find my own way. That's very poetic, and eventually I did. I am. But what would've been the harm in bringing me out to a powwow in his home community? What would've been the harm in talking to me as a teenager about where I'd come from, what he'd been through to get where he was? That's what we've been doing the past thirty years, isn't it? Couldn't we have started earlier, so I wouldn't have been so damn confused as a child? So lost. So unsure of myself. I don't know. It's hard to reconcile to this day, the understanding, the lack of understanding. But we make choices as parents because we want what's best for our children, and if we make those choices with love, which my parents did, then maybe that's all that matters. Whatever confusion I had, whatever journey I'm on this late in life as a result, well, that's my journey.

This recontextualization of my childhood has altered how I view myself as a Cree person. I want to seek out a Cree Elder, someone I know and trust, and find out my Cree name when I'm ready. I haven't done this yet. But the fact that I haven't sought out this experience does not make me less Cree. I have not attended a sweat. The anxiety that I live with has prevented me from doing so. I don't like being in confined places, and I don't like being in heat. I've had panic attacks from both. One day, I hope to overcome those fears, attend a sweat, and experience the benefits many of my friends have described from participating in this important ceremony. The fact that I've not gone into a sweat (I've sat outside to support others) does not make me less Cree. I've felt the vibrancy and peace of being out on Black Water. I've felt an indelible connection to Norway House, to the land, that I struggle to put into words. The fact that I've traversed the same lakes and rivers Dad did as a child does not make me more Cree. That the Chief put his jacket over my shoulders to welcome me home does not make me more Cree. I've learned a lot from Dad over the years, as we've worked to heal our relationship and ourselves, but still, his idea of being Cree differs from mine. He's a minister and a recognized Elder, something he is very proud of. I'm a writer and a father to five children, something I am very proud of.

WHAT IS CREE identity? There isn't one Cree identity. There are as many Cree identities as there are trees in the forests that line the rivers that lead me home when I visit Norway House and Black Water. There are as many Cree identities as there are Cree people.

Cultural appropriation has been in the news lately. It's good that people are aware of it, are talking about it, and are having mostly intelligent conversations about it, especially in response to asinine, disrespectful dismissals of it. That conversation has brought about an even more nuanced question: Can one Indigenous person appropriate the culture of another? This, too, is a question of identity.

In 2019, Tanya Tagaq, one of Canada's most prominent and important recording artists (and a damn fine writer and artist), boycotted the Indigenous Music Awards along with other Inuit throat singers known as the Arnaqquasaaq Collective because a Cree singer's debut album, which included throat singing, was nominated for an award. Throat singing is not a Cree art form. It's been practised by Inuit women since, as Dad would say, "before time was." Tagaq's contention was that the Cree singer had appropriated the art form, and the boycott prompted a debate over whether Indigenous People could take one another's cultures. The executive director for Winnipeg's Manito Ahbee Festival said that she didn't believe cultural appropriation was possible within the Indigenous community. The question "What is Indigenous identity?" can become "What, exactly, *is* the Indigenous community?" Is there one community? Saying there is seems to be saying there is one Indigenous culture, one Indigenous identity. Of course this isn't true. If I plan on writing a story about a Mohawk poet, I need to do the same work that I would expect a non-Indigenous person to do. I can't write that story simply because I'm Cree.

All this to say, there are different Indigenous cultures, languages, and communities across Turtle Island. We are not pan-Indigenous. There is not one Indigenous identity. When Dad said to me, "How am I going to say, 'Well, now I'm going to teach you to be an Aboriginal person'? You are," he meant that he'd wanted us to find our own way, that he'd hoped by living a certain life, he would model that for us rather than impose it upon us. And that changed things for me. How I viewed myself and my life then; how I view myself and my life now.

The story I've told countless times about the journey my father and I have been on for the past thirty years to heal our relationship, understand each other, and help me understand myself is somehow new, and somehow not. Because despite Dad's contention that he was showing me how to be Cree simply by living his own life as a Cree person, the truth is that he wasn't there often enough during my formative years to model it. What was his life, anyway? All those years I struggled in the 1980s, where was he?

"I don't think you've been a good father to me," I said to him, sitting on that couch in our basement. I didn't understand where he'd been. Maybe I couldn't have. I never knew why he wasn't around. Was it me? There was so much I didn't know. Not only about where he'd been, but about why he and Mom weren't together in the first place.

WHEN I FIRST started writing professionally, I began to do public speaking. If you want to get your work out there, it's a required activity. The audience changes depending on what kind of book you've written and who it's for. I have a diverse catalogue of literature, but most of my books are education-focused. I visit a lot of schools, do professional development sessions with teachers, and get asked to the odd literary festival. There are other events too—grand rounds at the Health Sciences Centre here in Winnipeg, the Marjorie Ward Lecture at the University of Manitoba, a Skype session with the Hospital for Sick Children in Toronto, and more. I've done prison visits as well, working with both adult and juvenile inmates—unsurprisingly, the majority of these people have been Indigenous. (A discussion about that would require another book.) My point is that because I have a diverse catalogue of writings, I've spoken to diverse segments of the population. But for the most part, I talk about the same thing.

This is partly out of necessity. You just can't come up with a hundred different presentations for a hundred different visits, no matter who your audience is. Dad has had a similar experience in his ministry. When he was in Melita, he was responsible for three towns; Melita was just his home base. Every Sunday, he gave a sermon at Melita, then Napinka, and finally Tilston.

"You didn't give three different sermons a day, did you?" I asked.

Dad shook his head vehemently, as if the idea was insane. "No, it was the same one. I mean, it wouldn't be verbatim, but the sermon was the same."

Maybe I've taken this to the extreme. Since I did my first event as a published author in December 2008, I've spoken to tens of thousands of Canadians, and I've mostly talked about the same thing: me and Dad. This isn't because I've nothing else to say. From presentation to presentation, I'll frame the story differently. But it has always been the jumping-off point for a broader discussion about reconciliation, cultural reclamation, Indigenous representation, mental health awareness, and so on. As the years have passed, the story has evolved. I've learned more because Dad and I have continued to talk. As I've learned more, the story has changed. I feel this is of benefit to the audience, but selfishly, it has also been of benefit to me. I've formed a deeper understanding of Dad and of myself. My identity has become stronger. I've become more self-confident (although I don't think I'll ever walk into a hospitality suite at a literary festival and feel I belong there).

Because I'm continually learning, things I've said in the past have sometimes turned out to be wrong. That's not to say it wasn't my truth at the time—it's just that I remembered things differently, or Dad remembered things differently, or I interpreted things differently, or the documentation was inaccurate, or I was never told at all and was forced to come to my own conclusions based on the information I had on hand. Sometimes I had no information. Sometimes it wasn't me coming to conclusions but others, based on the same information or lack thereof.

It was 2010, early on in my writing career, and I was at one of my first literary festivals. I was excited. Somebody had actually sought me out and asked me to talk about my graphic novel. They paid for my flight, put me up in a hotel, even paid me an honorarium. It was an entirely new world. Jill had come with me—one of the few times she's accompanied me to a literary festival or on a speaking tour. (I can't blame her. When I leave home, she has five children to look after. Life's busy enough when we're both in Winnipeg.) I think she came because I was still dealing with the long-term effects of a nervous breakdown I'd had earlier in the year. I needed the support. I didn't think I could walk more than a block without her holding my hand.

In the basement of a rather pretty rustic library, I talked about how I became a writer and how I came to write *The Life of Helen Betty Osborne*, and in order to frame that, I talked about my life and Dad's. Back then, I'd no idea why Dad and Mom had separated. I had baseless assumptions, but these weren't something I was about to share. Instead, I talked about the ten years my parents were separated, my life with Mom and my brothers, and how I really got to know Dad for the first time in the 1990s. Getting to know him shaped my life, my career, my writing, I explained. After I'd finished talking about my own journey and the story of Helen Betty Osborne, I felt good. I'd been dreadfully nervous beforehand, but all in all, things went well. I'd given a fine presentation, and a reasonable crowd had come out. I took questions when I was done.

"Why were your parents separated?" somebody asked.

I didn't think it was anybody's business, and besides, the audience only needed to understand that they'd been separated, and that my dad was Cree and my mom was English, Irish, and Scottish. That was it.

"I don't think that matters," I said.

Discussing the impact of his absence had been enough. The impact was germane to my talk. The reason why they'd separated was not.

"He was probably a drunk," said somebody near the middle of the room, off to the side.

I can still picture the man. I can still hear his words. Everybody else in the room had heard them too. The ensuing silence spoke volumes. If the same thing happened today, I would say something in response. I would have a respectful conversation with the man, showing him the kind of respect he'd not afforded me or my father. As it was, I sat silent. Stunned. I don't remember if there were any further questions. My memory stops at that moment. At those words. He was probably a drunk. A drunken Native. It's a tired stereotype that existed in 2010, still exists today, and most certainly existed in the 1980s. A stereotype that, I am ashamed to admit, I believed as a child growing up in River Heights.

There were several stereotypes about Indigenous People, and because they were all we had, we bought into them. These widely held beliefs, these unwavering images of a people, were true. They had to be. If they weren't true, then what was? When I was a kid, nobody said otherwise. Think of *Room* by Emma Donoghue. Jack is raised within the confines of Room. He's been imprisoned in a shed from birth. To Jack, Room is all that exists. He believes that Room is the sum of existence because he is never presented with evidence to the contrary. So if I were to tell you that all Indigenous People are drunks, and you were never given proof of anything different, how would you know that an Indigenous person was not a drunk? You wouldn't. You couldn't. The way you saw every single Indigenous person would be informed by the "truth" you'd been fed, and your actions would also be informed by that "truth." The sober Indigenous person becomes the anomaly, not the norm. That's why stereotypes are so damaging, and why truth, real truth, is so important. But it's a big job. These stereotypes were prevalent, and still are today.

My son played tackle football when he was eleven years old. We were living in the West End at the time—a neighbourhood I never would have gone to when I was younger. Our catchment was St. James, so Cole played for the Rods. Other teams in the city were the Broncos, Mustangs, Wolverines, Nationals, and Nomads. The Nomads were the team from the North End. During our game against them, a parent leaned over to me and told me with a chuckle that everybody called the Nomads the No Dads. The implication was that kids in the North End—kids who were predominantly Indigenous—didn't have fathers. Wait a minute. My father didn't live with us when we were growing up, and we're Indigenous. Does that make the stereotype true?

Jill and I had our bachelor and bachelorette parties on the same night. We were at different bars to start and the plan was to meet up at the end of the night. I forget what bar we went to, but I do remember that I had too much to drink. I never made it to our rendezvous spot. I ended up puking in the bathroom and getting kicked out of the bar. My night ended early. Does the fact that I drank too much make me a drunken Indian? Why or why not? Does it change things that I was drinking for pleasure, rather than to mask pain? Anxiety? Depression? I've done that, too, before I learned how to deal with my mental health issues in a more productive way. If somebody had seen me walking down the street, stumbling, would they have assumed I was a drunken Indian and judged me for it? Would they have changed their mind if they stopped and talked to me, found out that I'd been dealing with anxiety and thought alcohol was the only way I could numb the terrible sensations in my body, the terrible thoughts in my mind?

Maybe Dad drank leading up to the separation. Maybe he drank after. He has not had a drink for over thirty-five years, so which grade does he get, the low or the high? And just because he drank before, does that make the stereotype true?

LeBron James is a phenomenal basketball player. Serena

Williams is a phenomenal tennis player. Black people are better at sports than white people. Korean women are better at golf than white women. Japanese people eat sushi and read manga 24/7 (which actually sounds pretty awesome). When I call a taxi, I know that a dude in a turban is going to pull up to the curb. First Nations people are all drunks. And hey, how many Indians does it take to screw in a light bulb? None, because they'll get the government to do it for them. And yet, Trayvon Martin did nothing wrong. Emmett Till did nothing wrong. Japanese Canadians who were sent to internment camps did nothing wrong. Sikhs aren't Muslims, and Muslims aren't terrorists. First Nations children did nothing wrong, are still doing nothing wrong. J.J. Harper and Helen Betty Osborne did nothing wrong.

Just because somebody happens to fit a stereotype, that doesn't mean the stereotype is accurate. Larry Bird was pretty good at basketball. Tiger Woods isn't bad at golf. And a white Canadian woman named Brooke Henderson has won a few tournaments on the LPGA Tour. I love sushi (vegan sushi, but still), and I don't eat fried bread. The KKK is a terrorist organization. Dylann Roof and Stephen Paddock, they're terrorists as well.

This argument could come across as glib, considering the gravity of white supremacy, of mass shootings. What's the point, anyway? Why make the leap from a seemingly innocuous stereotype like "Black people are good at basketball" to Trayvon Martin, the unarmed Florida teenager who was shot to death in a gated community because he was Black and shouldn't have been there, I suppose. (He should have; he was visiting relatives.)

First, the disenfranchised—Indigenous, Black, LGBTQIA2S, disabled, and so on—carry with them, across generations, similar experiences, similar traumas, and similar resiliencies. George

Zimmerman was acquitted. So were Raymond Cormier and Gerald Stanley. (The latter is the man who shot Colten Boushie in the back of the head.) Second, stereotypes escalate into something far worse. Indigenous women are easy, and they like to party. That was the widely held belief in The Pas in the 1960s and 1970s, and it led to white men cruising around town looking for Indigenous women. On November 13, 1971, four young men found Helen Betty Osborne and asked her if she wanted to party with them. When she refused, they kidnapped and murdered her.

That man in the library basement, who muttered under his breath but not really under his breath that Dad was probably just a drunken Indian, developed that belief from somewhere. If he'd been fed it through popular culture or learned it from his parents or friends, how do we change that belief? Who's going to do it?

I should have. I know that now. Silence is complicity. In 1991, the *Report of the Aboriginal Justice Inquiry of Manitoba*, in addressing the death of Helen Betty Osborne, concluded that the men who killed her showed a "total lack of regard for her person or her rights as an individual." But the co-commissioners, Senator Murray Sinclair and the late A.C. Hamilton, associate chief justice of Manitoba, went further: "Those who knew the story and remained silent must share their guilt." In The Pas, there was a conspiracy of silence. Many residents in the town knew who'd murdered Betty, and yet nobody came forward for almost seventeen years. If even one person had spoken up immediately (because the killers bragged openly about their act of hate and violence), the men would have been brought to justice sooner and eased a family's, a community's, pain. I don't think it's an overstatement to say that they must share the guilt of the perpetrators. They could have done something, and chose not to.

Silence *is* complicity. It just is. It was then, and it was that day in
the library. Because I didn't speak up, that man left my session
believing that Dad was a drunk because he's an Indian, and all
Indians are drunks. It was probably not the first time he'd said
something like that, and maybe he still feels that way. If he has
kids, do they feel that way too? How do we undo that sort of
damage?

That happened a decade ago. I've thought about it a lot
since, and I'm still not sure what I would say if I had the chance
to do it over. Usually, we think of the clever things we should
have said in an argument long after the argument has ended. Not
this time.

I don't think I said anything to the guy who called me a
"fucking monkey" either. What could I have said to him? What
could somebody else have said to him? What could somebody else
have said to the guy in the basement of the library? What would
you have said? If you saw me staring at the man, my mouth agape,
stunned to silence, hardly able to breathe, would you have said
anything to stick up for me?

Dad was the superintendent of the Manitoba Indian Education Board from 1979 until 1982, about a year after he and
Mom separated. From 1982 until 1985, he was the coordinator
of student support services and education programs for the Winnipeg Core Area Training and Employment Agency. To finish off
the 1980s, he was the director of education for the Island Lake
Tribal Council. From the time Dad started working as director
of IMPACTE, he'd been busy changing the face of education in
Manitoba and Canada for Indigenous People. He was working
long hours. He was travelling to communities, perhaps still sleeping on floors, trudging through snow with socks on his hands so
he wouldn't be late for a meeting, flying in torpedo-shaped planes

that felt like they might crumble into dust during turbulence. Meanwhile, Mom was home with three young boys, raising us single-handedly, growing tired of doing it alone.

The lazy Indian. That's a stereotype I've mentioned before, and it's a common one. I'm not saying Dad's a hero. He would be the first to admit that he made mistakes. He didn't feel that he deserved to be asked to leave the family, but he recognizes why he and Mom needed to be apart. He had work to do to set things right. He needed to determine his priorities. You see, Dad and Mom separated, in the end, because he was working too hard at his job, and it took him away from his family, both when he was gone and when he wasn't. That doesn't sound too lazy to me.

I don't know. Sometimes I wish I could go back in time and lay this whole argument down for that man. It would be a "drop the mic" kind of moment. I could have literally dropped a mic too. But most of the time, I've come to accept that you can't change the past; you can only learn from it. Dad has said that to me on several occasions. When he was younger, maybe he wished he could go back too. Then again, maybe not. He's expressed to me that he doesn't regret how we were raised, only that he didn't teach us the language. I know he didn't want to be away from me and my brothers, from Mom, but I also know that this time apart, however painful, was necessary. And that's all I know about how those ten years felt for Dad—that they were painful—because I can never bring myself to ask him, and he hasn't told me. Even then, what happened, happened. There's no going back. Not for him, and not for me.

Still, the past *has* changed for me. Sure, the clock didn't strike thirteen, opening a portal into the past through the backdoor of a flat like it does in my favourite book, *Tom's Midnight Garden*.

Nevertheless, my life had been framed by a belief about how I'd been raised, and I know now that belief was mistaken.

"How am I going to do that? How am I going to say, 'Well, now I'm going to teach you to be an Aboriginal person'? You are."

In that same conversation, Dad expanded on this.

"I've never said that I was going to teach you to be Aboriginal, but I've also never said that I don't want you to know who I am."

His belief was that the way he lived his life—how he conducted himself, how he interacted with people—told his children, "Here is what my dad is." I can see how this approach to parenting, this approach to relationships generally, was informed by his own upbringing. All the knowledge that Dad was gifted until he was nine was Indigenous knowledge, but nobody—not his father, not his grandfather—ever came out and said that. Nobody ever said to him, "We are living like Cree people." It was just the way they lived. It was just the things they knew. And within that way of living and knowing, there was a value system that was handed down from one generation to the next. That value system was what made my father Cree. It was not how he dressed. It was not how he looked. It was how those values were innate in his life.

"It's not trying to *be* something; it's trying to *live* something."

How do I reconcile this new truth? How do I reconcile that I view my childhood through a different lens now, through a renewed perspective, when I'm not sure anything would have changed no matter what happened? If I really was raised to be non-Indigenous like I thought I was, shielded from my indigeneity because I was better off not being Indigenous in the 1980s in Canada, if things had happened for me the way I thought they had, I still would've ended up right where I am now. Somebody who was raised to be a good human being and is inherently Cree. Dad's intent was to model how to live a Cree life, not impress it upon me, and for me to develop a sense of identity through that example. He just wasn't around enough to do that modelling, and I needed it to counter all the stereotypes that had become ingrained in me.

MITATAHT-PĒYAKOSAP
(ELEVEN)

Eric's boat is one of many pulled onto the shore at the end of the highway, where the car ferry *Gilbert Laugher* stands ready to take the next load of vehicles across the river to Highway 373. Sometimes there's only one car waiting. At the moment, there are none. Eric backs his truck up close to the boat, a large aluminum vessel with forward and middle wooden thwarts that Dad and I will sit on. We load our things into it. Eric's brought three fishing rods, a cooler, a rifle, and a stadium seat cushion for Dad. Dad has his lunch kit, and I've got my backpack filled with the snacks I bought at the gas station, anxiety medication, my grandfather's old Kodak Vigilant Six-20, a digital SLR camera, and the minnows. My plan is to savour the day, to stay in the moment, but at the same time, to take photographs so that I can document the trip for myself and my kids.

It's a beautiful day. The river is peaceful with only subtle undulations; the serenity I found on the highway has carried over to the water. The sun shines down unimpeded, the sky is a brilliant blue, and there's a smattering of cumulus clouds hovering over the treeline.

I feel grateful for it as I help Dad into the boat; he'll sit at the front so the land reveals itself to him first. Grateful, and something else I can't articulate. Protective, maybe. I appreciate the North I've come to experience. I'm keenly aware that it's a place others don't know. It won't be long until we'll pass by the spot on the west shore where thirteen years ago a community member filmed Mistapew, or Bigfoot. It was a predictably grainy video, lasting all of forty seconds, and it's all that most outsiders know of this area. The closest they'll experience of the prettiness of it is listening to a song by the Weakerthans appropriately titled "Bigfoot!" I love that song, but it's not the same as standing on the rocky shores and looking out over the land. It's not the same as breathing in the air.

Eric drives his truck across the road and parks it, and I watch him walk back over to the boat. He gets in and sits at the stern, by the motor. He pulls a cord violently to start it up, as one would start a lawnmower, and after a few tries, the motor coughs to life. I'm tasked with pushing the boat away from the rocky shore. I brace my feet against the rocks, grasp the side of the boat, and ease it away from land. As it starts to drift out into the river, I clumsily get in, just narrowly avoiding falling into the cool water.

We ease out. The river is at least one hundred yards wide. There's a thick rope that stretches from one side of the water to the other and guides the ferry on its repeated round-trip journey. When the ferry stops to pick up vehicles, the rope sinks below the surface. In the winter, the ice road opens up just beside where the rope is now.

To our left, to the south, the river would take us back to Norway House if we were so inclined. I look from the right to the left, and for a moment, I stare off in that direction. The wide water, like the road, becomes smaller the closer it gets to the horizon, and I can't help but imagine a group of canoes full of relatives, my relatives, heading back to the community after spending months on the land together. I can't help but feel the way they must've felt, their excitement knowing that their family and friends were waiting for them on the shore with outstretched arms and food set for a feast. I can't help but look at Dad, sitting at the front of the boat in his special chair, and picture him younger, just a boy, even though a man in the eyes of his people, in the canoe with all my relations on the journey home. And how comforting to know that whatever direction they went, whatever direction we go now, it's home either way.

FOR THE MAJORITY of Dad's time away from us, he was the director of education for the Island Lake Tribal Council, but in the summer of 1991, he was called back to save a struggling BUN-TEP. When I wanted to talk to him after that party when I was in grade nine, he'd already moved to Brandon, a two-hour drive west. So not only were he and Mom separated, but he wasn't even living in Winnipeg. I'm not sure if I saw him less or more, but it hurt. It felt like a death knell for their relationship. I think every child in a separated family wants the family to be whole. For the ten years they'd been apart to that point, I'd always hoped Mom and Dad would get back together. How could they if they were moving farther away from each other?

I spent the rest of that year wondering what good it had done to tell Dad what I'd told him. He came to visit on the weekends, and we were talking more, but he was still only coming home on the weekends. I knew what he did for a living, but what he did for a living was keeping him away from me. It didn't matter if I saw him just as much I had before, or even if our times together were more frequent. Where there was once an emotional distance, there now stood a physical one.

Near the end of the school year, in 1992, we learned that Dad was getting an honorary doctorate from Brandon University, the first of two he would receive, and we travelled there as a family to watch the ceremony. We stayed at the Royal Oak Inn. Mom was in one room and we boys were in another. Mike, Cam, and I were getting ready for the event when Mom knocked on our hotel room door.

"Can you boys come into my room for a minute?"

I couldn't read her. Had something happened? We filed out of our room and into hers to find Dad standing there. Mom went to stand beside him. She asked us to sit down on the bed. We did. I was freaking out. My heart was jackhammering. My palms were sweating. Everybody was quiet. It's a rare occasion when parents call all their kids into one room and have them sit down. It's usually bad news. They looked at each other for too long, then looked at us.

"Your father and I are getting back together."

I picked Mom up and spun her around, but everything after that is a blur. This moment, which changed my life, has planted a flag in my mind and taken ownership of that day, leaving very little room for anything else. I have it on good authority, however, that a degree-granting ceremony did take place. There is photographic evidence. I know that we made fun of the blue hat

Dad wore with his gown; we called him Papa Smurf. I'm beaming in the pictures, as if my smile's going to burst off my face. Dad is standing on stage, under the bright, hot lights, receiving the doctorate. I can picture him there, but I can't remember the words he spoke. Luckily, I have them right in front of me. "The great tennis player Althea Gibson said, 'No matter what accomplishments you make, somebody helps you.' In the accomplishments I've been able to make, somebody has helped me as well. As a matter of fact, wonderful people have helped me: my friends, my colleagues, Elders, my family . . ."

My family. This meant something new now. I think I suspected that my parents would reconcile at some point, but I don't know if I believed it would *actually* happen. Mom and Dad want to keep a lot of these details within our family, and I want to respect those wishes, but I can say that to me it seemed quick and easy. They weren't together for years, they'd been getting along really well, and then—*boom!*—the separation ended. I think I can also say that while it seemed quick and easy, it was not. It took work, and it took time. Years. Almost as long as they were apart, Mom and Dad were working to get back together. When they were sure they were ready, absolutely sure, they called us into that hotel room and told us the news. Best. Day. Ever.

BY AUGUST 1992, Dad had moved home, having found a job at Red River Community College as their first dean of Aboriginal education and institutional diversity. I didn't know until recently that we almost went to him instead. Evidently, as the youngest Robertson, I'd been left out of the decision-making process, but Mike and Cam were asked if they would move to Brandon. They refused. All their friends were in the city. I don't blame them, but I would've gone anywhere if it meant living with Dad again. As it turned out, I did live with him in Brandon, but only for a week.

This weird thing happened to me in the summer between grades eight and nine. In the eighth grade I was relatively tall and quite overweight. I was teased for being fat, which was a deterrent for admitting to anybody that I was Native. I didn't want to be teased for something else too. When I started grade nine, though, I was almost unrecognizable. I'd grown several inches and had shed all the baby fat, just as Mom promised I would. I was over six feet tall and would've been a prime candidate for the basketball team. I loved playing ball. I shot hoops every day on the court beside Brock Corydon School. But I didn't try out. I might've made it. I might not have. Tryouts were early in the school year, and at that time, I still wasn't used to my new body. I was lanky, uncoordinated, and awkward.

In time, my brain caught up to my body, and by the summer, I was intent on trying out for the junior varsity team at Kelvin High School. The problem for me was that I'd never played on an organized basketball team before. I'd never developed any real basketball skills or knowledge. All I'd done, up to that point, was shoot around at Brock Corydon. The only people I'd played against were a bunch of older Jewish guys who were friends of the Greenbergs, our neighbours. I destroyed them, but what would happen when I played against kids who'd been playing way longer than me?

In the summer of 1992, Dad was wrapping up his stint as director of BUNTEP and getting ready to begin work at Red River come September. He knew about a one-week basketball camp at Brandon University that he thought would be good for me if I wanted to make the team. At the beginning of the week,

they assessed your skill level, and depending on how you performed, you were placed into one of a number of groups, from
beginners to more advanced players.

I decided to go. For the basketball camp. For Dad. I couldn't
wait for him to be home, and this seemed a good way to bridge the
gap. Mom drove me out in the Pontiac Acadian on a Sunday,
the day before camp started. Dad was waiting for us, sitting on the
steps of the house on 20th Street, where he rented a basement
suite.

I wish I remembered more about staying there. As it stands, I
have moments in time. Like Cam's old strobe light, they flash in
front of my mind's eye.

The basement suite was dark. It had wood panelling and a
floral-patterned couch that Dad slept on for the week. There was
a kitchen, a living room, and a bedroom that I took over. At night
when Dad was asleep, after we'd eaten supper and played cards or
watched a movie, I'd lie on the bed with my Sony Walkman and
listen to *Simon and Garfunkel's Greatest Hits*. I listen to it today
because it reminds me of then.

Time works mysteriously. The days after I'd found out Dad
and Mom were getting back together inched forward, reluctant
to go anywhere. They'd passed slower still when Mom signed me
up for the basketball camp, because I knew I'd be staying with
Dad. And then, the week in Brandon was over like a VHS tape on
fast-forward. I wanted a pause button. When Mom came to get
me, it felt like she'd dropped me off, driven around the block, and
come back to pick me up again.

I left Brandon missing Dad instantly, but I didn't leave feeling
more Indigenous than I had before. I didn't leave feeling proud
of who I was, or all of a sudden wanting to go to a gas station and
buy a Native Pride baseball cap. Real change isn't fast, even if it

feels that way. Dad wanted to model what it meant to live a Cree life rather than impress it upon us, and he was going to be in a position to do that now more than ever, but it would take years of work from both of us. And if we're being honest, those things weren't top of mind, if they were on the radar at all. I can't say that as Mom brought me back home to Winnipeg after my seven days with Dad, I thought, "Hey, I'm feeling more Indigenous now, and it's not as bad as I thought!" I was too busy revelling in the fact that I was going to live with Dad again, and adjusting to it. That week in Brandon was a trial run. It went well, but it was really just the prologue to the story of us. Even if I was conscious of Dad's presence and its impact on my indigeneity, a lifetime of one experience isn't undone by a week of another. And there was so much shit—so many falsities about Indigenous People that I'd been exposed to—that needed to be purged.

I might've known what Dad did for a living, I might've known where he was going after he dropped me off at the basketball court in the morning, but he didn't fit into what I knew to be an Indigenous person. He was an anomaly. Not one of those sad people with tattered clothing and scraggly hair staggering down Portage Avenue, smelling like piss and looking for money to buy a bottle of Listerine. The only thing that smelled nice about those people was their breath. No, Dad dressed in a suit. His apartment was modest but clean. He didn't even have one drink the entire week I was there. He had short black hair that he styled with a comb, without any product, and it stayed in place. He didn't stagger—he strolled.

While it hurts to write the description of that stereotype, it was something I believed. It was something that a lot of kids believed. It was something a lot of adults believed. Nobody, not kids or adults, asked that man staggering down Portage Avenue what had brought him to stagger down Portage Avenue. Nobody, not kids or adults, would care to admit that there were more people like Dad—educated, hard-working people who were making a difference. We've thrust Indigenous People into the darkest corners of this country. Many have beat the odds and found success, but many have not. All are human beings.

Dad arrived home in September 1992, and his influence, the modelling that he talked about in our interviews together, was gradual. For the first years of Dad's return, the transformation in me wasn't obvious. I was just happy he was back. It was weird to have him living with us, to get up in the morning and find him sitting on the couch in his green robe, working on a crossword puzzle, but it was also exhilarating. It's like I had to rub my eyes and blink for the first while just to ensure that I wasn't seeing things.

At school, nothing much changed. I made the junior varsity basketball team despite annihilating my ankle near the end of the second tryout. My foot was more or less dangling from my leg. When I got out of my space boot, I went through rehab and then joined the team mid-season. The Kelvin Clippers were in the city division. We played against John Taylor, Sisler, Daniel Mac, Tech Voc, Gordon Bell, Churchill, St. John's, and Elmwood. We dreaded the away games where we had to travel north. Daniel Mac wasn't so bad (that was the West End), but St. John's (the North End) and Elmwood (*in* Elmwood)? That's where all the Natives lived. The kids on those teams were all Native. The kids on those teams, because they were Native, were most certainly rough and dangerous. They were probably in gangs. Those games couldn't end fast enough. Those games felt longer than they should have, like the summer days waiting for Dad to come home. When the buzzer sounded, we almost didn't stop running—just grabbed our bags and got out of there. Fast. Before the Native kids could beat us up, take our shoes, do something to us, just like we expected them to do.

Never once did we stop to consider that those kids didn't play rougher than we did, and that no matter how much they'd lost by (we always beat Elmwood by a lopsided score), they lined up, shook hands, and told us we'd played a good game. I played on the varsity team for two years, and the trips into the North End never became less intimidating. There was block white lettering on the roof of an autobody shop that became visible as you crested the bridge towards Dufferin Avenue. It served as an unofficial greeting to the area, reading, "Welcome to the North End." In my mind, the words sounded like they'd been recited by Darth Vader.

I remember hanging out with a girl later in high school, somewhere close to grade twelve. I wouldn't say we were dating, but we'd seen each other a few times. We talked on the phone a lot in the few short days we were something more than friends. I sang "Frying Pan" by Evan Dando to her using the extension in Mom and Dad's bedroom. Then she asked me the same question as the girl at my locker in grade eight.

"Are you an Indian?"

I told her, even as I lay on my stomach on the bed now shared by my parents, one of whom was Cree, that I wasn't.

"Oh," she said. "Then what are you?"

I had to be *something*. Certainly not white. I was too dark. I waffled. I didn't know what to say if I wasn't going to tell her the truth. We were silent. Silence on the phone is so much worse than silence in person. At least in person you can communicate with your eyes, with body language. I was going over all the things I could say, the explanations for my pigment.

She offered her own. "Are you half Black?"

I had a shaved head at the time. I had black hair and dark brown skin. It was around summer. My skin, as a result, was as dark as it could get. It wasn't a crazy guess. Certainly not malicious. I laughed. I laughed at the question, but she thought I'd laughed at her, and that was enough. Right there, she broke it off—whatever "it" had been. She called me shallow, and right after I'd sung to her. Singing to her had taken a lot of courage; I have a terrible voice. But maybe it *had* come across as shallow, reacting the way I did. It was nervous laughter, but she wouldn't have known that. And I didn't tell her. Maybe I was shallow and ignorant, and it was safer that way. At least she didn't know I was an Indian. I was still doing what I had done my entire life: hiding.

Dad was home, but that didn't matter. At least not yet. I'd had the epiphany the night I met Vince. I thought differently, or at least I imagined I did, but when the chips were down, I acted the same way I had ever since I'd learned I was Indigenous. Acted, then reacted. When anybody asked me what my cultural background was, I lied about it. When I was asked if I was Indigenous, I always denied it. Vehemently. I wore a Cleveland Indians baseball cap because Chief Wahoo's bright red skin was redder than mine, as though to say, "Don't look at me—look at him!" When my friends told Indian jokes, I laughed along, as though to say that exact same thing. A mantra.

"Don't look at me—look at them! I'm not one of them!"

The jokes weren't about me. The racial slurs weren't about me. You know them. I know them. I knew them. I said them, because what if I didn't?

At night, I would stare up at the ceiling, at the square of moonlight cast against it by the opening in my heavy blue curtains, and take it all back, promise myself that things would change tomorrow. I'd throw the hat out. I wouldn't laugh at the jokes. I'd say, "Yeah, I'm Native," and not care what anybody else thought. Then I'd break that promise. I'd go to school the next day with my hat fastened tightly around my head like a vise and smile through the jokes and the slurs as broadly as Chief Wahoo.

MITATAHT-NĪSOSAP (TWELVE)

The moment we hit the water, I notice something different in Dad. He has more energy, and it's been building since we arrived in Norway House. Gone is the unsteadiness in his gait, the sunken eyes, the drawn and weathered face. It's unmistakable. Sitting there, with only the water and the land and the blue skies in front of us, his shoulders are broad, his chin is up, there's more colour to him.

People used to be shocked when I told them Dad was in his seventies. "What? No way. He looks like he's sixty." I liked those reactions; it made me feel like he was immortal, like he'd never age. But in the last couple of years, he's looked properly his age—early eighties—and it's made me realize that he's just like the rest of us. He's aging, and now it's happening too fast.

So I can't stop looking at him. I don't want to look away from him. It feels as though, in the moment, this is why I came here. I watch the wind whip his salt-and-pepper hair, and those tired eyes are newly infused with childlike wonder. They search from left to right, from the waters to the sky, wide and passionate.

I take pictures of him so that when this is all over, I'll still have the Dad I see now. So that one day, somebody might ask me how old he was in these pictures and I'll say, "Eighty-three," and the person's jaw will drop. "What? No way. He looks like he's seventy." I'll like that reaction.

At first, I use my grandfather's camera. I struggle to get the settings right on the sixty-year-old contraption before taking one photograph. I struggle, but I like that it requires work and patience. You can't take a burst photo and choose from fifty-seven pictures taken within three seconds. You have to wait for the right moment, the exact right moment, because there are only eight exposures per roll. When you find the moment, you can't let it slip away.

I take one picture of Dad. Weeks later, back in the city, I will discover that I captured something special: Dad, turned to the side and perfectly in focus, his eyes searching but determined, nothing but water and forest ahead.

I'm more generous with the SLR camera. I snap picture after picture of him, mostly the back of his head because his attention is focused on what's in front. He doesn't pose. He hates having his picture taken. On his eighty-third birthday, I tried to take a selfie of us, and he stuck a spatula in the way. (I posted a picture of me and a cooking utensil on Instagram.)

An eagle soars above, pronounced against the perfect blue, and I take a photograph of Dad looking at it. I don't have to wait to get this photo developed; I check it right away. Dad's to the left, his navy windbreaker offering a third shade of blue in contrast to the water and the sky, and the eagle is in the shape of a lowercase *m*. It appears just inches away from Dad's right, framed by a string of cotton clouds and a green Velcro strip of birch and pine trees.

THERE WAS A progression. We didn't go on this journey of healing, of discovery, right out of the gate as soon as Dad moved back in with us. At first, having a father who was around all the time was a novelty for me. Like when I buy a new album, and it's all I listen to for months. When I get a Spider-Man T-shirt and wear it to death, until Jill has to steal it away just to put it in the wash. It was exciting to wake up early on a weekend morning and not have to wait at the door for Dad to pick me up for a round of golf at Cottonwood. We would eat breakfast together at the kitchen table before the sun rose, trying not to wake anybody up, only our chewing breaking through the silence. Then we'd sneak out the door and get on the road to make our seven o'clock tee time. We got to the golf course at the same time we would've before, but those quiet moments, those seemingly mundane moments, were the ones I cherished most at first.

My brothers and I were raised by Mom. She'd raised us well. Aside from one time when our neighbour Dorothy caught us riding our bikes through her pile of topsoil and called us monsters, we were good kids. A *Winnipeg Free Press* reporter, Val Werier, was another neighbour. He wrote a column about kindness and mentioned how I had shovelled his sidewalk in the winter and refused to let him pay me. Terrible from a business standpoint, but pretty nice, I suppose. Now another parent had arrived late in the game to help raise us.

In the winter of 1995–96, my friends and I frequented The A, a dance bar on Portage Avenue. (I'd started to make friends in high school, partly because of my involvement in sports, partly because of my slowly building confidence.) One night, a girl drove me home, and we parked outside my house, talking until almost four in the morning. This didn't sit too well with Dad. He appeared on the front step in his green bathrobe, looking annoyed. I didn't have to come inside. I was nineteen. But I said goodnight to the girl and left to get in shit with Dad. Even then, getting in trouble with him was pretty cool. Everything felt like we were making up for lost time.

"I have a dad who I can get in shit with? Awesome!"

We played golf together at Cottonwood every weekend. We talked more as Dad's presence became less of a novelty, when I knew he was there to stay. There, on the couch in the morning with his crossword puzzle. There, beating me at golf no matter how far ahead I was after nine holes. There, in the basement with me, watching our favourite movie: *The Fugitive*. There, in the stands at all my basketball games, home and away.

The last time Dad ever played basketball, it was with me. We were on the outdoor court at Queenston School. Dad was wearing a white T-shirt, navy shorts, and a knee brace. We were playing one-on-one. I couldn't beat him at golf, but I could beat him at basketball. He took a wrong step and messed up his knee, and never played again. It was the first sign, to me, that he was, in fact, aging.

Sometimes I visited Dad at Red River Community College, met the people he worked with, came to understand what he did for a living. He told me about IMPACTE, BUNTEP, and his time at Island Lake Tribal Council. On his desk, there was a white coffee mug with bold black lettering that read "World's Best

Boss." Dad was the boss. People worked for him. He had a nice office with a window, and an assistant who set his appointments, answered the phone, typed out his letters.

It's hard to quantify the impact this had on me. It's difficult to articulate. The more I learned about Dad, the more I met other Indigenous professionals like him—people with master's degrees and PhDs—the more I began to realize that there was a lot I didn't know. And that what I thought I knew was wrong, inaccurate, misinformed. It wasn't my fault; I was a young man. A youth in the eyes of most people. But there was a point when, if I continued to believe what I had my entire life when there existed evidence to the contrary, it would've become my fault. There would've come a time when my beliefs ceased to be the responsibility of others and rested solely on my shoulders.

And it wasn't just that I met so many Indigenous People who didn't fit into the stereotypes I'd been force-fed. I talked to Dad's friend Strini about this, probably on the fairways of Cottonwood Golf Course. We were discussing stereotypes. When I saw an Indigenous person who fit into the expectations I used to have, an unkempt man staggering down Portage Avenue desperate for change, what did that mean now? Because although my eyes had started to open, not all Indigenous People were professionals with degrees and offices with big windows and fancy mugs and neatly pressed suits. As I got to know Dad better, day after day, month after month, year after year, as I talked more to him about his life, what he did now, what he'd done before, how he'd grown up, my eyes were opening, but not to a utopian society. There really were Indigenous People struggling.

Strini did what Dad has been known to do: he told me a story. He'd been walking downtown one day, he said, and saw somebody like the unkempt man I'd just described. Somebody who fit into the stereotype of the drunk, poverty-stricken Indian. The man was sitting on the ground and extended his hand towards Strini, asking for money. Strini had some food on him. He sat down beside this person and shared his lunch. Talked to him. Listened to him. Worked to understand how he'd come to be where he was. And in so doing, the man became more than just a stereotype. He became a human being.

Not many people would do something like this—I suppose it could be viewed as a radical act of reconciliation. When I lived in the West End in my late twenties and early thirties, I used to see a guy begging out front of the 7-Eleven. I'd buy him food, and from time to time, I'd talk to him. I'm sure others have done something similar, as much as I'm sure many have not. That's not judgment; it can be uncomfortable for people. Not many people do this even when it's not so radical, when the opportunity presents itself to have a respectful dialogue with another person.

In 1998, I was at a restaurant in downtown Winnipeg, having dinner with my girlfriend at the time. We were going to eat, then head over to Portage Place for a movie. The restaurant was busy. We were surrounded by conversations wafting through the air, the sound of cutlery scraping against porcelain, waiters navigating the obstacle course of circular tables. In the midst of all this, in the collision of smell and sound, one particular conversation rose above all else, pushed through to find its way to our table. There were two people sitting across from each other—an old man and an even older woman. By appearance, they were affluent. The man was making fun of an Indigenous person, spitting racist words out of his mouth while he delicately cut his steak, a napkin unfolded and resting on his lap. It wasn't just what he was saying, but how vociferous he was about it, how he said the words. Making fun of this unnamed, faceless person by imitating the way he spoke. You know, the way that Native people speak.

I scanned the restaurant. There was no doubt: others could hear the unrelenting monologue. People were ignoring him. People were glancing over, annoyed, but not annoyed enough to say something to him. People were snickering at the exactness of his send-up. It was hilarious dinner entertainment. I looked at the man, at my date, the man, my date, quietly making a decision I'd not made before. I wasn't laughing along. I wasn't hiding. And I could be wrong, but I don't think my girlfriend wanted me to talk to the man. She might've thought nothing good could come from it, and she would've been right, in a sense. I wasn't going to change the man's mind. Still, I got up from my table and, with the man continuing to tell his jokes with that familiar Native drawl, walked over to his. The words stopped, and with them the impression. The couple put their cutlery down. Their forks chimed against their plates.

"Can I help you?" the man asked.

"Yeah," I said, my heart pounding. I have always hated confrontations, and still do. "What you're saying is really offensive, and I'd like it if you stopped."

"Oh," the man said, "I was just joking. He's somebody I work with."

"Do you think he'd appreciate you talking about him like that?" I asked. "Because I'm Native and I don't."

"Well, I'm sorry," the man said unconvincingly.

I went back to my table and looked at my girlfriend apologetically. My heart was still pounding. It would continue to pound until we left the restaurant. I ate the rest of my food clumsily because my hands wouldn't stop shaking. The whole room was suddenly quiet. The conversations had stopped. Even the forks and knives were quiet in their connections with food and porcelain. I heard the man muttering to his female companion, but I couldn't make out the words. A contrast from just moments earlier. Then he stood up, placed his napkin atop his plate, and approached our table.

"Since you so rudely interrupted my dinner with my mother," he said, "I thought I would interrupt your dinner too."

"Sure, okay," I said, and put my fork down as he had, hiding my trembling hands under the table.

"I want you to know," he said, "that I wasn't being racist. I'm not racist. I work with, and know, lots of Natives. That's how my friend talks, and I don't appreciate you talking to me like you did."

"Are you done?" I asked. "Feel better about yourself?"

"Yes," he said. "I do."

"Okay, enjoy your dinner," I said.

He returned to his mother. My girlfriend and I didn't talk. It was quiet enough, at that point, for me to hear the man speak to his mother as he placed his napkin back on his lap. There were no more jokes. No more impressions.

"Can you believe that boy?" he said, then grunted. "Some people are so sensitive about things. He's probably an artist or something."

The previous exchange deserves a footnote, because nobody actually says that in real life, right? "I'm not racist. I have lots of friends who are _____." It's a cliché of the extreme variety called the friend argument. It comes in many forms, and each one of those forms is an incredibly lazy way for people to explain themselves when they've said something prejudicial. An excellent illustration that cuts to the heart of the absurdity of the friend argument comes from British comedian Sean Lock, who stated, "I'm not a murderer; some of my best friends are alive." In short, if people attempt to worm their way out of responsibility for saying something offensive by using this tactic, they are in fact racist, homophobic, transphobic, sexist, et cetera. Rest assured, the silver-haired man in the expensive suit said that exact thing to me. Ipso facto, he was racist. He was right about one thing, though: even then, twenty-one years ago, I considered myself an artist.

Looking back, I'm not sure I thought much about what I was doing before I did it. I was at my table, feeling upset. Pulse hammering, chest burning, limbs trembling. Then I was at the old man's table, engaging with him respectfully. I suppose I could've waited until he was done eating, but I've changed my mind about that. He'd not considered others when he started to tell his "jokes." My point here relates to how I felt, walking from the restaurant to Portage Place, to a movie my girlfriend and I never saw. We ended up sitting outside the theatre in relative silence before going home early. It bothered me, what the man had said. It bothered me at least as much as what had *not* been said by anybody else in the restaurant. Why hadn't anybody else stood up and said something? Why had the burden of action been placed on my shoulders? I'm not saying I'm a hero. Far from it. I interrupted a guy's dinner to tell him he was being offensive. We all have that capacity. What's pertinent to this discussion is that action against the behaviour, rather than supporting it by either participation or inaction, was something new to me.

ON JANUARY 14, 1998, two days after my birthday, Grandpa
Eyers passed away from amyotrophic lateral sclerosis in Melita. A
few days earlier, he'd been taken to the hospital because he woke
up without the use of his legs. It shouldn't have been a surprise,
but it was. I don't think you're ever really prepared for a loved
one to die. I was sleeping. Mom put a hand on my shoulder
and shook me awake gently. Cam had moved out, but he'd been
called home to hear the news. I followed him, Mom, and Dad
to the basement, to Mike's room. Mom woke him up too. We
huddled together in a circle, shoulder to shoulder, and Mom told
us that her father had died. Earlier in the night, the reverend had
come to see him. Grandpa—Mickey, to people in Melita—had
a resigned look on his face, the reverend said. Peaceful. At the
end of their brief visit, Grandpa shook his hand with what must
have been the last of his strength. The reverend told this story
at Grandpa's funeral days later. He said it was how he expected
Grandpa to go: like a gentleman.

For years, I had a man in my life that I knew well and looked
up to, and I think all of us boys became gentlemen because
of the influence Grandpa had on us. When I think about it, his
influence was kind of like the influence Dad wanted to have on
us when we were children. Grandpa showed us how to be gentlemen by being a gentleman himself. He never sat us down and
said, "This is how to be a gentleman." He just was, right up until
the end, when he had every right to be bitter and angry at the
hand he'd been dealt. Instead, he lay on the hospital bed, in pain
and fear, and shook his reverend's hand with quiet dignity before
dying. I had this role model growing up, even though I missed
my father. I don't think it was a coincidence, then, that in the year
of my grandfather's death, Dad began to have the sort of influence on my life that he'd always intended to have.

"Was there a point," I asked him, "when you decided it was time to bring us to Norway House?"

He talked about how he'd seen us grow up with a strong attachment to Melita, where Mom was raised. He'd seen how close we were with Grandpa and Grandma, Mom's parents. With Auntie Joan and Shayne. We knew the town well, and over the years, we came to know the people in it. There was a reason we didn't have the same attachment to Norway House. But it wasn't the reason I thought for most of my life: that going to Dad's home community would be admitting our indigeneity, and so was off limits. On the contrary, I'm certain we would have gone if things had been different between Mom and Dad. If they'd stayed together. But this wasn't the case. Norway House, during the 1980s and most of the 1990s, was a community I never knew existed. By contrast, I knew Melita like the back of my hand. The haunted house in the farmer's field near the third hole of the golf course, the dirty magazine Shayne hid on the roof of the school, the cemetery where Grandpa buried his dog, Great-grandma's pink house, the water tower.

"Did you ever get jealous of us going to Melita so much?" I asked.

Dad paused. He adjusted his baseball cap. He leaned on his cane so that he could pull himself forward, sit at the edge of the couch, closer to me.

"I would have liked for you to meet my parents," he said. "You knew Nana a little bit, but not really."

"I don't remember her," I said.

"I know."

I wish I had known her. I wish I had really known her, like Dad did. Maybe I would've been different if I'd seen her more often, if she'd lived a little bit longer. I think a lot about something he told me at my office in 2019: "If there was some way that I could identify those things that I was able to do that were somehow the strength of the people from Norway House, the Cree people. That I inherited some strength, some kind of attribute, some kind of value from my community that gave me the ability to adjust to the things that I had to adjust to." I suggested that maybe the answer wasn't so general, that while he'd certainly inherited attributes from the people of the community, he might have had a more direct influence: his mother.

"Maybe it's just like you said, that influence of role modelling," I offered. "Your mom made transitions from the residential school to the community and from the community to the city, and did so, I would think, in dealing with tough losses."

"Oh, yeah," Dad agreed. She'd lost her sister, Maggie. Her children, Frederick, Effie, and Cameron. Her husband, James.

"From all accounts," I went on, "she was this loving, generous, strong woman. That's probably something that would have had an influence on you."

Dad would've liked for me to meet his father. James Robertson was somebody I never got an opportunity to know. My knowledge of him, my connection to him, exists solely through the stories I've been told about him. One night, deep in the cold of a northern winter, he was walking to work when he came across some friends. They were in a Bombardier B12, kind of like a snow bus on tracks, and decided to play a joke on my grandfather, pretend to play chicken with him. The machine got too close, his friends lost control, and James was killed instantly. It was December 22, 1962. He was fifty-five. Dad was only twenty-seven. This, unfortunately, is the story I know best.

Dad would've liked for me to meet his brother, Cameron. Cameron had been sick his entire life. He'd struggled with his health in a way that I cannot relate to, but he'd done so with good humour, courage, and the sort of strength that Dad talked about inheriting from the community, from Nana. "He was a fun kid. He was just good to be around," Dad said. "You remind me of him." We would've got along, Dad told me. He died in 1971 from kidney disease, six years before I was born. He was thirty. Dad was thirty-six.

Why did he reference these family members? Even if he and Mom had stayed together, I never would have met them. I think that if we weren't able to meet his family, the ones who had passed away, he wanted us to know where they, and he, had lived. Where they, and he, had grown up. In so doing, we would know them in some small way. And we would know him better than we had before.

"I wanted you to see that our life was different," Dad said. "I wanted you to see where I played, where I lived. You'd been to Melita, and now you'd see Norway House. You'd be able to see in your mind 'This is where my dad came from.' And you'd be able to answer questions like 'How did he get from there to here?'" Dad leaned back into the couch. He placed his cane beside his leg. "I'm not a rich man, and I didn't come from a rich family. But my siblings and I have done well. We've done well because we had caring parents who wanted their kids to be successful. The same thing your mother and I wanted for you and your brothers."

It's funny. I remember how much Norway House felt like home to me the moment I stepped out of the van and onto the ground outside the York Boat Inn, but my time there with family is a blur. I know we went places, and I know those places well because I've been there many times now. But I can't really picture us there. Only the memory of the Chief taking the jacket off his shoulders and placing it onto mine remains entrenched in my mind.

"Welcome home."

I don't even have the pink Hilroy scribbler I wrote notes in throughout the trip (ironically, so that what has happened now wouldn't happen). I wish I had it. I wish I could read through the notes and be transported back to 2000. It's frustrating. The trip meant so much to me, so why can't I remember it? I called Mom, and half an hour later, I was holding a square red binder with a puzzle design on the front—yellow puzzle pieces with purple asterisks littered all over, and a red heart at the centre outlined in thick purple. A photo album of pictures from those three days in Dad's childhood home.

IN WRITING GRAPHIC novels, I have come to understand and appreciate the power of images. When I'm reviewing a graphic novel page, I ask myself if an illustration says all that needs to be said. If it does, I take out the words. When you place images in sequence, it is an incredibly effective way to convey meaning or tell a story. This method of storytelling is called sequential art. Comics and graphic novels are forms of sequential art. This is the way we used to communicate with each other before we had any words. Mom's photo album, with the pictures arranged in sequence, one after the other, is a story, a work of sequential art. Those spaces between the pictures, or illustrations, are called gutters. Readers become storytellers by existing within the gutters, because it's where they make connections between images and fill in the blanks. They animate the still pictures into a moving, living story. When I looked at the photo album, at the pictures of my family's trip to Norway House, memories came flooding back as though I'd always had them, as though I'd never lost them. A picture gave me a moment, and the album gave me a memory of home.

THE FIRST PICTURE was of a vehicle on the dirt road leading into the community. The door to the vehicle is open, and there's a rez dog sniffing at the rear bumper. Beside the photograph, Mom's note reads: "Trip to Norway House, Fall 2000. We rented a van. Don, Bev, Michael & Andrea, David, Cameron went on the trip."

The first thing I noticed was that the van wasn't as large as I remembered it. I thought we'd gone there in a cargo van or something similar to that. In reality, it was a seven-passenger bur-gundy Dodge Caravan. The picture below that photograph was of a plaque at the Fort, looking out over the Nelson River. The plaque read: "Norway House was the crossroads of the northern transport network of the Hudson's Bay Company during most of the 19th Century. Three structures—the Archway, jail and pow-der magazine—survive as tangible reminders of the importance of this place in western British North America." It goes on to explain, in detail, each of the three structures.

We walked through the ruins, starting from the bridge that leads to the West Island and heading down the embankment towards the Archway. We walked together while Dad told us more history about the area than any plaque could. His words carried us over the slanted and rotting but somehow sturdy boardwalk, which groaned and tilted its way over the water, then back towards the land. We walked through the Archway and finally to the Gaol, where we each tried to peer inside to see what a jail would've looked like back then. Appropriately, it was locked. I wouldn't know what was inside until nineteen years later, when Cole risked losing his phone by sticking his arm inside and recording the cramped space. The windows, if you could call them that, each had one bar, leaving just enough space for the arm of a thirteen-year-old child.

We crossed the street, and I wasn't sure why at first. There wasn't much to see. It wasn't a historical site like the Fort. There was no creepy old jail, stone ruins, or old boardwalk that hinted at danger. Instead, there was a large, empty parking lot that was surrounded by an abandoned hockey arena, a baseball diamond, and the water treatment plant. We stood in the parking lot and surveyed the area, trying to make something significant out of a baseball diamond and a hockey arena. But it was significant for what used to be there, rather than what was there now. It was where Dad had finished the eighth grade.

When we left, we drove to where Dad went to school for the first time. That school was gone too. And again, I was left to imagine what it would've been like for him there, what it would've looked like, what he would've learned. There's no photo album for Dad's childhood. No square-shaped book with connected yellow puzzle pieces on the front. No deep red heart outlined in purple. No notes to add context to the photographs. The picture of his young life would become clearer only over the next nineteen years, as he told me more about growing up on the land and in the community. The only way to keep those memories—to preserve them under a thin sheet of cellophane, to ensure they never fade away—is to continue to have those conversations, to continue to listen and share those stories with others, with your family, with your children. This is the way it has always been.

We toured the community. Stopped by Auntie Flora and Uncle Oliver's place, where we posed for a family photo on the steps of their house. Mike's standing between Mom and Dad, his arms around them. I'm sitting beside Cam on the front step, my arm around his shoulders. My auntie and uncle bookend the Robertson clan at either side of the steps.

We spent time at the old church at the southwest end of Rossville. We walked around the church, then inside it. We sat in the wooden pews, watching dust dance in the air, our bodies awash in multicoloured light filtered through the stained-glass window. Dad stood at the front of the pews, and I wonder if he was thinking about the day he came back to the community after all that time away. I wonder if he was picturing Nana almost in tears in the congregation. He probably wasn't. I believe him when he tells me that he doesn't think much about the past. I've been forcing him to, and he has seemed to enjoy the process, but he'd still rather not. It's *me* picturing Dad as a young man at the front of the church, *me* picturing Nana almost crying. Dad doesn't think enough about the past, and I think about it too much.

The pictures of us on Robertson Bay close out the section of the photo album reserved for our first trip up north as a family. We had no relatives who lived there anymore. These loops, these pockets of land off the main roads, are where relatives settle, where they live in close proximity to one another. Auntie Flora and Uncle Oliver live in another area of the reserve, next to other prefab bungalows where Oliver's side of the family lives. Flora is the only one of Dad's siblings who remained in the community.

We followed Dad to the shoreline, where large flat rocks nestled up to the land and offered us sure-footed platforms to the water's edge. Rocky surfaces are indicative of the Boreal Shield. Though rife with vegetation (white and black spruce, balsam firs, jack pines, and bush for miles), those surfaces make agriculture nearly impossible. Funny, right? The reserve system was put in place to encourage First Nations people to adopt an agricultural lifestyle, yet they were forced onto lands unsuitable for that way of life. Rocky areas, like the ones all over Norway House, with poor soil and steep slopes, are just not conducive to farming. It would be like giving people pickaxes and hard hats with little flashlights on them and telling them they'd be mining in their new community but neglecting to mention that there was nowhere to mine. Neglecting to mention or intentionally omitting. Semantics. The result would be the same: "Sorry not sorry, but thanks for the land, and here's five dollars. No inflation."

All those flat, rocky surfaces, like the ones on the shore where Dad used to live, were good for playing on. He used to jump from rock to rock and try not to land in the water, but if he did, it was no big deal. When he wasn't jumping on the rocks, he was swimming.

Dad pointed out where he and his siblings used to swim; the rocks they used to jump on; the spot where he caught the barge that used to take him and the sand from Rossville to where the hospital was being built; the path the skiff took when it brought him and his parents home from church on Sundays. All of the things you could see from there, he pointed out to us.

He was excited to talk about his life back then because he'd never told us about it before. It was as though he was waiting to be here, at his home, to tell us. I was excited to hear him talk. Back then, I'd never heard these stories. Nineteen years later, I've heard them several times and they still feel new.

The pictures of us on Robertson Bay are all by Little Playgreen Lake. There are photographs of Dad standing with Mike, talking to him, pointing out over the water. There's one of him and Cam walking from the grass towards the path that leads to the shore. We pose on the rocks, our backs to the lake, the RCMP detachment visible in the background, and beyond that, Rossville. In these snapshots, the community looks far away, and I can hear Dad's voice: "I wanted you to see where I lived . . . You'd see Norway House. You'd be able to see in your mind 'This is where my dad came from.' And you'd be able to answer questions like 'How did he get from there to here?'"

Here, from Black Water to Robertson Bay. Here, from Robertson Bay to Rossville. Here, from Rossville to Phoenix, then on to British Columbia. To Melita. Brandon. Calgary. Here, to Winnipeg, Manitoba. Here, all the way back to Norway House, where it all started, with my family staring out over Little Playgreen Lake as though all of that still lay ahead, as though I could feel water splash against my pant leg from Dad as a boy, falling off a rock and into the lake.

MITATAHT-NISTOSAP
(THIRTEEN)

The water breaks off into smaller arms that weave around tiny islands, then find their way back together, only to break apart again at the emergence of more pockets of land. At times, we rush through these tributaries, but Eric also sees fit to shut the engine off every once in a while, allowing the boat to drift towards the shore. He brings us to places where others have stayed in the past, to names and dates chiselled into stone. He tells us the story of one inscription: *Joe A. May 8, 1943.* Joe Apetagon. He was too young to enlist in the army and fight in the Second World War, so instead, he stayed on a small parcel of land surrounded by the swift waters of Nelson River.

Eric points out dwellings where community members still live, connecting the present to the past. I can feel history course through these watery veins; there is a palpable sense of familiarity that I find hard to ignore. I see the same things over and over. Eagles soaring overhead towards nests that bulge at the top of trees. Muskrats announcing their presence with slick bodies shimmering from the sun's generous light. And there are so many beaver lodges that Eric asks over the roar of the engine, "You know what they call those, eh?" Before Dad or I can respond, he says, "Native Holiday Inns!" It sends us all into a fit of laughter.

As lunch approaches and we near Black Water, Dad's expression changes. It's subtle. He'd been scanning the area reflectively, maybe reminiscing about the past, picturing himself canoeing these waters with his father seventy years ago. I want that to be a tradition that is kept. I want to bring my children out here and look back fondly on this day, right now. I wonder what Dad's thinking about. I wonder if the images of him and his father are as clear as I hope the images of today will be for me. Whatever Dad was doing before, he's searching now, and not for memories.

He and Eric talk about how the water levels have gone up since he was a boy. It's made the trapline hard to find, the path towards it uncertain, the landmarks he and his father would have used in the past washed away. There's an urgency we haven't felt before. The three of us fall silent. The only sounds are the water splashing against the bow and the engine churning at the stern. Dad continues to examine the area and his memory, trying to match the two and find a connection.

Then the narrow passage we've been boating on opens to a large body of water, and Dad perks up. Eric shuts the engine off, and we glide towards land straight ahead. Before that, the water changes colour in a straight line, from the Cambridge Blue we've been travelling on to a deep and dark shade of midnight. Black Water, a literal description of a beautiful phenomenon. Farther out, there's water where long reeds sway above the surface like a full head of salty blond hair. That place is called Hairy Lake. Things are named in this way. Dad points towards the land, at a dark boulder in the middle of a clearing that's only just visible through a thin grove.

"Is that it?" I ask.

He nods.

IT WAS EARLY September 2001, in the morning, and I was twenty-four. Emily, our oldest daughter, wouldn't be born for another two years. That meant it was just me and Jill. We had eaten breakfast and were likely doing nothing of significance. Just hanging out. I can't even remember what we did with our time before children. What an alien concept. Jill might've been updating her LiveJournal or talking on the phone with her best friend, Leora. I might've been playing *Ghost Recon* on my PlayStation or writing on Grandpa Eyers's old electric typewriter. These were all frequent activities. I remember getting my wisdom teeth out around this time and spending a day on the couch playing video games and eating ice cream.

You'd think, because it was the weekend and the morning, that we'd be well-rested. Typically we were. We were able to sleep in back then. But we weren't rested; we were exhausted. And whatever we were doing, it was probably being done as a distraction. We'd been up most of the night worrying because early in the evening, Mom had called to tell us that Dad was in the hospital. She didn't want us to worry, didn't want to make a big deal out of it, but how could we not? Over the phone from Dad's hospital room, as calmly as she could, Mom filled me in on what had happened.

Earlier in the day, Dad had been golfing with his friend Stan Bird. Things were going fine. Dad was probably hitting almost every fairway (like he does when he plays against me), probably taking several shots to get out of sand bunkers (which have always been his Achilles heel), and probably hitting every putt without inspecting the break or the slope of the green. After the ninth hole, Dad had to go to the bathroom. But it was more than that. He'd started to sweat, and he felt weak and cold. He thought he had diarrhea. That trip to the outhouse wasn't his first.

On the tenth tee, he remarked to Stan, more offhand than anything, "Geez, I'm really going to the washroom quite a bit."

Stan brushed it off. "There's a flu going around."

Dad brushed it off too. He kept feeling awful, kept going to every bathroom on the course, but that didn't stop him. He and Stan played the whole eighteen.

When he arrived home, Mom was there. She wasn't supposed to be. For some reason, she had decided to come home two days early from visiting Grandma Eyers in Melita. She said she had lots to do. Holly, her future daughter-in-law, had a bridal shower coming up. Cam's wedding was in two weeks. But really, she still can't explain why she left Melita on Friday rather than Sunday and got home just before Dad returned from golf.

They greeted each other, but not for long because Dad needed to use the bathroom again. For the first time since he'd started out at the golf course, he went to a real bathroom, not an outhouse. White porcelain. That's when he saw it. He hadn't been having diarrhea. He'd been shitting blood. A round of golf typically lasts about four hours, which meant he'd been bleeding internally for at least that long. Mom insisted that they go to the hospital. Dad was opposed.

"I don't need to go to the hospital," he told her. "I'm not going to the hospital. I'll rest and I'll be fine."

Dad is stubborn. I know it. I've seen it. But Mom's stubbornness, especially when it comes to her family, puts his to shame.

"No, you're going," she said.

Dad, with clammy, pale skin. Dad, trembling and weak. Dad, looking like he was going to pass out at any moment. He still complained the whole way. He wasn't happy with Mom for making him go.

"I don't have to," he said repeatedly.

But Mom didn't waver, even when she overshot Victoria General Hospital.

"See?" Dad said. "That's a sign I'm not supposed to go. I told you. You don't even know where you're going. We may as well just go home and I'll go to bed."

Undeterred, Mom pulled a U-turn. She drove right up to the emergency room doors and guided Dad into the hospital. At triage, Mom hurriedly explained what was going on.

"I have a doctor's appointment next week," Dad said, remaining defiant.

"Mr. Robertson," the triage nurse said, "I don't think this can wait that long."

They took him right in and he was immediately given blood transfusions. After the transfusions his internal bleeding stopped, and Dad was admitted for observation. Sometimes, the doctor explained, it just stops and the patient is fine. Dad had been bleeding from his intestines—they couldn't tell exactly where— but then it just . . . quit. By that time, it was late. When it seemed Dad was in the clear, Mom picked up the phone and called me and my brothers. After making the phone calls, and having saved

Dad's life, she went home for the night. There was nothing more she could do. Her expectation was that she'd get up in the morning, freshen up, have breakfast, and then head over to the hospital to see how Dad was feeling. Those expectations were not met. Early in the morning, well before she'd intended to wake up, Mom got a call from the hospital.

"Mrs. Robertson," the nurse said, "your husband's bleeding has started again. You should come now."

They were going to take him into surgery. Mom raced to the hospital and was able to see him before he went under the knife. The doctor told her that he would try to save enough large intestine so Dad wouldn't need a colostomy bag. This proved to be a difficult task in itself; Mom learned afterwards that Dad had been bleeding so much the surgical team couldn't even see where it originated.

When Dad was in surgery, Mom had a chance to call everybody again. Jill and I abandoned whatever it was that we were doing and were in the car within seconds. Victoria General Hospital was by the University of Manitoba. A twenty-minute drive from our house. It couldn't have been the Grace Hospital or the Health Sciences Centre, both closer. Every minute felt slower than the last, no matter how fast I drove, how many stop signs I rolled through, how many yellow lights I ignored. I wanted to run the red lights too, get other cars to stop by flashing my brights and honking my horn. They'd know it was urgent. I wanted a police escort—anything to get me there faster. Luckily, there were no red-light cameras back then. I might've gotten a few notices in the mail. All the way there, Mom's voice repeated in my mind: "Your father's in surgery."

When we finally arrived, we found Mom waiting for us inside. Cam, Mike, Andrea, and Holly were there too. Dad was out of surgery and in recovery. We filed into a private room and sat together, waiting to see him. So much of that day is a blur, but I remember those first moments, sitting in uncomfortable brown leather chairs. Maybe they were comfortable. Maybe it was the waiting that was uncomfortable.

We went to see Dad in small groups; I went with Andrea, Mike's wife, but I don't remember that. I had to be reminded of it by Mom. On the way to his bedside in the ICU, I was told by a nurse that he was lucky to be alive. She said that if he'd arrived even five minutes later the night before, he wouldn't have made it. That's how much blood he'd lost while golfing. It hit me that one more drop would've been it for him. For our relationship. For everything I had left to learn. By then, I'd only just started to scratch the surface.

Five minutes. I'm listening to a song right now, "Byegone" by Volcano Choir. It's 4:23 long. If Mom and Dad had arrived at Victoria General Hospital the length of that song later, Dad wouldn't be with us today. He wouldn't have been with us for the other two weddings that year (Mike had already got married in July). He wouldn't have been my best man. He wouldn't have golfed with us boys at Clear Lake every August, first thing in the morning. He wouldn't have been there to laugh when a squirrel took Cam's muffin on the eleventh hole, two years in a row. He wouldn't have travelled with me to The Pas and then Norway House while I conducted research for my first book. He wouldn't have come with me to Ottawa when I won the Governor General's Literary Award for *When We Were Alone*. He wouldn't have been the star of that week in the nation's capital, according to people I've come to love, including writer and illustrator Julie Flett and novelist Cherie Dimaline.

There are countless "what ifs" that have kept me up at night when the day he got sick comes into my mind. They are often uninvited. What if Mom had hit a couple of red lights? What if she'd driven a bit farther before realizing she missed the turn? What if she hadn't come home from Melita at all? Sure, Cam had his wedding, but even Mom isn't sure that's why. And really, shouldn't she have wanted two more days of peace before the two weeks of chaos leading up to the wedding? This isn't a knock on Cam's wedding. *Any* wedding, and the time leading up to it, is chaotic.

I don't know if I'm a religious man. I've wrestled with belief, with faith, ever since I heard about God at Sunday school. Ever since I found out that one day I was going to die. Sometimes, what might be construed as coincidence intervenes.

In the mid-2000s, Jill and I were in financial trouble. I'd made plans to meet a friend of mine for lunch, but I had no money to pay for food. On the way to work that morning, I was going over potential excuses, ways to tell my friend that I couldn't make it. An excuse that didn't sound like an excuse. I'd been walking to work for exercise, and my path took me through a rougher area of the city, down Cumberland Avenue. Immediately after crossing Balmoral Street, I looked to my right and saw a neatly folded ten-dollar bill on the road, right against the curb. Just enough for a hot dog and chips at one of the food trucks on Broadway Avenue. How could that money have been there, and right when I'd been lamenting that I had no way to pay for lunch? Another day around this time, a co-worker of mine and devout Christian came into my cubicle and tapped me on the shoulder. I turned around, and he shook my hand. I felt something in my palm. He'd slipped me two hundred dollars.

"I can't take this," I said, but he wouldn't let me give it back.

"You need it," he said, and he was right, but he couldn't have known that.

Mom's coming home in time to save Dad's life seems an enormous coincidence—so much so that to this day, I wonder if it was a coincidence at all. I wonder if it just wasn't Dad's time, and maybe, just maybe, the God he'd been preaching about since he was a young man decided to intervene. I guess I have more faith than I thought. Dad wanted to show me what it meant to be Cree by living his life that way. By showing me and then letting me find my own way. It's not hard to accept that this sort of modelling spilled over into a belief in a higher power and I'm only just realizing it now. I'm a slow learner, but as unbelievable as it might seem to me, it's all there. And it's not subtle.

Mom left Melita when she did. She arrived just before Dad came home from golf. What if she'd stopped in Brandon to grab an order of fries from McDonald's? She's always been a sucker for French fries. What if she'd blown a tire on the highway and needed to call CAA? What if she'd filled up her car at the Shell just outside Portage La Prairie? What if she'd forgotten something and had to turn around and go back to Melita, and at that point thought to herself, "Forget it, I'll just go home on Sunday"? What if, what if, what if? I've belaboured the point, but it's only because I still have this image in my mind of Dad coming home from golf, lying down because he was so weak and so tired, and falling asleep. He would not have woken up.

Once when Dad was a boy, he was jumping from boat to boat over the river water, and one boat drifted farther away. He missed the jump, fell into the water, and got sucked underneath the surface by the current. When he fought against it, he started to see what he described to me as the Yellow.

"They say that when you see the Yellow, like in a flash or something," he explained, "you're dying."

On that Friday, Dad would've closed his eyes, seen the Yellow, and passed away quietly in his sleep. Where would I be now if that had happened? I can't answer that. Thankfully, I don't have to. So many things went right after something had gone so horribly wrong.

When I got to the ICU, I saw Dad from across the room, lying under a teal-coloured sheet. I kept following the nurse. The closer I got to him, the more details began to present themselves. I wanted to turn back. The intensive care unit was circular, with the beds surrounding a central nursing station. I was twenty feet from him and started to feel dizzy. The circular room had started to spin. It was Dad. It wasn't Dad. He looked bloated. There were so many wires protruding from his body they looked like veins. They snaked across the bed and hooked into machines. A large tube was sticking out of his mouth, and his body was rising and falling in rhythm with a mechanical ventilator. Ten feet away. His eyes were closed. When the breathing machine rested for a moment before hissing back to life, he was motionless. The feeling left my fingers and toes. Numbness crawled across my entire body. The room spun harder. The lights got darker, then shut off entirely. I blacked out.

Before I collapsed, I'd felt my sister-in-law Andrea's arms around my waist. She eased me onto a chair at the central station. She or a nurse brought me a cup of water and told me to drink it. I don't know how long I sat there. Those moments remain a blur. I sat, sipped at the water, and stared at Dad. I tried to make him look like Dad. It wasn't working. I saw the wires, the breathing tube, the bloated body, the thin teal sheet, the green line that miraculously indicated a heartbeat, but I did not see my father. Not at first. Not for a long time. Not until after I was able to stand, walk to his bedside, and sit down. Not until I navigated my hand through the maze of wires and slipped my fingers underneath his palm. Not until I whispered, fearful that if I talked louder, he'd break apart, "Dad, it's Dave. I'm here." Not until I saw his eyelids, still glued shut following the surgery, quiver. Not until I felt his hand begin to close around my fingers. Not until he squeezed my hand softly, as though I might break apart too. It was Dad, and he knew I was there.

When this happened, I wasn't thinking, "No, Dad, don't die. You haven't taught me all you can yet. I have so much more to learn." To say that would be disingenuous. Clearly, things were changing for me. But my involvement in Indigenous employment, my interest in Dad's work, my accompanying him to events and conferences—these weren't things he pushed me into. I did them of my own accord. Looking back, I see that Dad's dream of influencing me was happening. I became involved with Indigenous employment not because he forced it upon me, but rather because of the influence his life had on mine. The modelling that he'd hoped would happen before I was born had been happening since he came back into our lives. As I sat beside Dad and held his hand, I thought something closer to "Don't go, Dad. We've had only ten years together."

I wanted more time.

I don't know what I said to him after those first words, telling him that it was me, that I was beside him. I don't know how long I sat there holding his hand. I have only images. The tubes and wires. Dad's chest rising and falling with the assistance of the respirator. The grey pallor of his skin. His eyelids glued shut. The colour of his bedsheet. The quiet of the room, hanging in the air like a chill. Dads were supposed to be invincible, weren't they? You were supposed to be invincible, weren't you?

BEFORE ALL THIS happened, Dad was overweight, but after he lost his large intestine, that changed quickly. I would say that what happened to him was a blessing in disguise, but given how much he has suffered over the years as a direct result of this incident, I know better. Yes, he eats better now than he used to, but he has to. He can't eat many foods. He'd take his large intestine over his slim figure all week long and twice on Sunday. I remember him at Cam's wedding, just days after leaving the hospital. I saw Dad force himself to attend the ceremony and the reception that followed by sheer will alone. Frail. Grey. Wheelchair-bound. The only true blessing in all of this was that it showed how much he loves us boys. I still remember, during dinner, watching Strini wheel Dad away, Mom at their side. She'd booked a room for them so they wouldn't have to drive all the way home late at night. The day had taken everything out of him, and out of Mom as well.

Jill and I were married in October 2001 at Westminster United Church in Wolseley. It was a cool autumn day, and the wind made the warm-coloured leaves swirl like miniature tornadoes on the steps out front of the thick wooden doors. Dad looked more like himself by then. He was thinner, still not his colour, but out of the wheelchair and walking, albeit for short periods before having to sit down. But if you didn't know him, I'm not sure you would've realized just how sick he still was. I often look at the pictures from Mike's wedding, when Dad was well, and compare

them with the pictures from my wedding, when he was not. Side
by side, the change is drastic.

I will, of course, always remember my wedding because of Jill.
Here was a young woman who couldn't stand me at first, who
wanted no part of a second date with me, and yet for some reason
had eventually agreed to marry me. I look at pictures of us, too,
without Dad. The one we chose to blow up is of me giving Jill a
piggyback on the steps of the legislature. We look like kids. We
were kids. If I placed a photograph of me now beside me then,
the difference would be drastic as well. I've got grey hair weirdly
bunched together on the top right of my head (that's where I
carry my stress). I'm a few pounds heavier. I usually have a pretty
decent beard for a Cree guy, only because I'm too lazy to shave
most of the time.

The time between me now and me then is almost twenty
years.

The time between Dad's pictures is three months. Ninety days.

Dad was my best man. Not just because Cam chose Mike
and Mike chose Cam, and I was like, "Screw you guys! Being
the emcee doesn't make up for it. I'll just choose Dad." He and
I were close. Since he'd moved back in, as one year passed and
another came upon us, we had become closer, and closer still.
We were talking more about his life, and because of that, I was
understanding more about myself. But we also just spent time
together, and I feel like that's as important. We went to movies.
We went golfing. We went for walks around the neighbourhood.
We laughed together. We teased each other. He would introduce
me as his baby or as Baby Huey, and then explain who Baby Huey
was. We cuddled on the couch watching sports. He was my father,
my best friend, and my counsellor. When Jill broke up with me
for one entire painful night, he sat with me on my bed and let

me cry on his shoulder. When Jill and I exchanged vows, it made sense for him to be at my side.

I will always remember my wedding because of Jill, and in those memories, there will be Dad. He will be standing beside me when I give my vows. He will look tired, but he won't sit down until he's supposed to sit down. He will shake my hand after Jill and I kiss, and he'll tell me how proud he is of me. He will stand up in front of the crowd at the reception and give the toast to the groom without any roasting. I will have no memory of what he said, only of watching him speak. I will try to stop myself from thinking, as I watch him say the things that I will never remember, that he shouldn't be there, because of the million little things that had to go right after something went so wrong. I will instead choose to believe that he was always supposed to be there. Mom was supposed to come home, for no particular reason. She was supposed to hit only the right number of red lights and stop signs, to go only so far past the hospital, to get him to the emergency room in time. He was not supposed to see the Yellow.

Dad wasn't out of the woods. We thought he was at the hospital, then he wasn't. We thought he was after the weddings, then he wasn't. He developed an infection soon after Jill and I were married and ended up having one last surgery. It was only near the end of 2001 that we finally knew Dad would be okay. Or as okay as he was going to be.

Dad has called us, my brothers and me, every New Year's Eve at midnight to wish us a happy new year. These calls have blended together, there have been so many of them. But that one, as 2001 turned to 2002, has defined itself from all others. Not that he said anything different. Just that he called.

"Hello, my son."
"Hey, Dad."
"Happy new year."
"I love you."
"Me too."

MITATAHT-NĒWOSAP
(FOURTEEN)

▬▬

The boat slides over the line, onto Black Water, and continues until the hull scratches against rocks on the shore. The
ground is blanketed with loose rounded stones and slopes up
towards the clearing. I get out before Dad and find a walking
stick against the rocks, a simple piece of driftwood, white and
smooth, but shaped so perfectly that it feels intentionally left
there for him. He accepts it from me, holds the wood firmly in
his hand, and uses it as we make our way to the clearing. I put
my hand around his bicep for extra support, but this small act
isn't only for him. I want to be as close to Dad as possible. He
doesn't shoo me away like he does when I try to kiss him on the
cheek just to bug him or cuddle him on the couch when he's
trying to watch a show. I decide that Dad wants to be close to
me as well.

He stumbles. I tighten my grip. Hold him steady. We continue forward, one step at a time. Eric hangs back. Dad digs his walking stick into the ground, and it secures itself between two stones. Another step. We're closer still. Before he puts a foot onto the grass, I glance back and see more than just the space between here and the boat, the steps we've taken over that short distance.

I think of a poster, of all things, taped to a cubicle wall under the flickering, mind-numbing glare of florescent lighting. You've seen the poster, I'm sure. There are two distinct sets of footprints on a beach, and then they merge into one. There's text over the image, little white letters. It tells the story of a man looking back on his life who recognizes that one set of footprints is his and the other is Creator's. The man notices that in harder times, there's only one set of footprints. He asks Creator where He was in those difficult moments, when he needed Him most. Creator answers, in what I have pictured in the past as an extremely awkward moment, that those were the times when He had carried the man.

Dad and I, well, our poster is a bit different. There are still two sets of footprints, and sure, let's say they're in the sand for the aesthetics of this imaginary motivational poster. On our poster, however, there is at first only one set of footprints. I'm a baby, and Dad is carrying me. Then suddenly, there are two sets of footprints, and they are far away from each other. Dad and Mom have separated. Dad's footprints are by the water, the place he likes to be most. Mine are by the boardwalk. There is an ocean of sand between us. A great expanse. Then slowly, assuredly, the footprints come together, until they're side by side. Dad and Mom have reconciled, and through that reconciliation, he and I have worked to heal. The footprints continue on in this way. And while neither one of us picks the other up, we support each other. I think of a poster, of all things, and footprints. Where they came from, and how they continue on, side by side, until arriving here. Together.

MEMORIES ARE FOOTPRINTS in the sand. They're defined one moment, but gone the next. The tide has reached out and pulled them away. You're left with impressions that you desperately try to keep. Some you can. Playing in a carport awash in green light. I look at the cracked concrete, at my clothing, my skin, my hands. I look up, see the green polycarbonate roofing. Some you cannot. I remember my childhood this way—in moments, not memories. I'm sitting in the carport. I'm running away from my bedroom, towards the living room, towards Mom. I'm getting my face painted like a clown's, a red-haired girl behind me, her face already painted. I'm wearing a beige shirt with burgundy sleeves, and she's got a green shirt with yellow lettering. I don't have glasses yet; she does. We're in a field. We drink that orange liquid sugar from McDonald's. I'm placing an injured bird into a shoebox and bringing it to a woman with glasses and short hair. I'm hoping that it will live. My childhood is this way. I carry it with me in moments, not memories.

I remember my time with Dad this way, from 2002 onwards. He retired that year as executive director of the Manitoba First Nations Education Resource Centre. My friend Nicole recently found a photo album from his retirement party. It was attended by colleagues, politicians, mostly family. Cousins (so many cousins!), his siblings, me and my brothers, Mom. I flipped through the album several times, but kept coming back to two things: I look thin and awkward, and I'm wearing a suit with an undefinable colour. If pressed, I'd describe it as olive green. If the colour wasn't bad enough, it's two sizes too big. It makes me look like a kid, like I'd snuck into Dad's closet and put on an old suit of his to play dress-up, pretend to be him. I look at the pictures and shake my head, chuckling at my twenty-five-year-old self. I look at pictures of Dad. He was sixty-seven at the time, but he looks younger than that. He looks young, and he's gained weight since the health scare in 2001. This won't last.

Year after year, because he's missing his large intestine, he's gotten thinner. There are times when I catch myself staring at him, making comparisons between him at that moment and the other Dads I've stared at. I can't change the past, Dad's right about that, but I jealously want more time with him, because I know, however gradually it's happening, he's slipping away from me. I've tried to push through my uncertain faith and pray for the most ridiculous things. For a large intestine to manifest itself within his body so that he can eat properly again, retain nutrients. If my co-worker can hand me two hundred dollars because God told him I was struggling, why can't Dad get his fucking organ back and stay with us, stop slipping away?

No matter how hard I try, it feels like too many memories are leaving with him. My time with Dad has been this way. There are memories that stubbornly refuse to fade. Memories that remain clear and indelible. I can remember them as though they happened earlier this week.

I'm in a hockey arena right now. Cole's in a camp. I'm sitting at a table by a large window, and the sunlight is warming my back. I'm home for the week from Clear Lake because I've been travelling too much for my writing and don't have enough vacation days to spend the week at the cabin with Jill and our three younger children. I was there on the weekend with my family, Mom and Dad, Cam and Holly, their two youngest kids. Every night, Cam and I sat by the fire. On Saturday, we were making videos of me feeding him a variety of things, then sending the videos, one by one, to Michael, because he wasn't there. (It's funnier than it sounds.) Later, Dad came to sit with us, and I showed him the videos in sequence (they got progressively more involved and outrageous). We didn't think Dad would be impressed, but he laughed harder than I'd seen him laugh in years. When I think of it now, it's like he's right beside me. I can see him. I can hear him.

There are moments, because memories have collapsed into these impressions. Dad leaning over his cane, two hands clutched around its handle, standing outside the open passenger-side door of his car, trying to find balance. He's been getting dizzier more frequently. We were sitting in a pew, and I kept glancing at him, at his eyes. They were glistening, close to tears. I've never seen him cry before. His oldest friend and adopted brother, Allan, had passed away. I think he saw his own mortality. I think I saw Dad's mortality. My eyes were glistening too.

Memories, moments with Dad are like this. They have been this way. Some are clear and indelible. Some exist only in impressions, as moments in time. Some are lost to me despite how hard I've tried to keep them, despite how important they are, each one of them. Some are lost, and I feel crushed under the weight of emptiness. Moments in time. However long or fleeting memories are, that's what they are. Dad's voice, in this moment, is clear to me. I can hear him talk to me, in one of the countless conversations we've had. He's telling me about time, what it means when you live in the city, and what it meant for him when he lived on the trapline, on Black Water.

"I tell people this, in terms of time: it is important because the animals have patterns. If you miss those patterns, like the muskrat run in the spring, then you're not going to get as many furs or eat as much. Work is like that in a way, even though it's different in the city. If you're late, then you've missed something."

We all share similarities. It's what makes us human. Recognizing our similarities, appreciating our differences, helps us to live as humans in a good way. There are similarities between the way we see time in the city and the way Indigenous People view time on the land. If you're late, you've missed something. But there are differences too. Western society is a slave to time. We crave immediacy. We've been conditioned for it.

"On Black Water," Dad said, "there is a calmness. You feel the serenity that the world brings. You see the ducks, you see the swift water, you see the fish. You go to this big lake and it's all right there in front of you. You see the houses along the shore where people live."

I don't know if you can feel the same kind of serenity in the city. The same calm. I don't know that you can just sit on a rock by the water, see all these things, and just . . . be.

I like to hear my anxiety medication rattle around in its plastic bottle while I walk; it lets me know that if I need it, it's there. I can take a pill, and in twenty minutes or so, the anxiety will subside. Presently, I've got about eleven minutes to go before the anxiety I'm feeling right now numbs out just enough for me to function a little better. The last time I didn't think about the pills in my pocket was on Black Water.

There is another kind of time, and I don't know where it fits right now. It feels like a hybrid of both. At once urgent and calm. It is reflective of my years with Dad since I saw him in the ICU and fainted. How I remember, how memories fracture into images, how they become lost. I know that our time together is limited. This felt less real ten years ago than it does now. Because our remaining time together is short, I want to spend more time with Dad, to create more memories and find a way to protect the ones I have. But being with Dad, despite the urgency of need, is calming. He is, to me, the embodiment of Black Water. It's as if the serenity he grew up around as a child is something he's carried with him throughout his life, and something I can feel. It's why when Dad is around, I think a little less about that pill bottle in my pocket.

Dad has talked a lot about the Elders. At one point, he told me that he wanted me to remember that in the Cree culture, we can't forget the influence of the Elders. When we stray from what we are, from who we are, when we lose these things, it's because we've forgotten that influence. We don't honour them now the way we did in the past.

Dad and a group of Elders have recently decided that they like the word "grandparents" better because there are so many interpretations of what it means to be an Elder. Whatever the word, one of the roles they had, and still have, is to be the keepers of knowledge, to pass it down to future generations. Doing this is a way to preserve knowledge of what and who we are, not to leave footprints in the sand but to etch them into stone. Historically, this wasn't done by literally etching knowledge into stone, but rather, it was passed down orally.

Things have changed. When I launched my first book, Senator Murray Sinclair acknowledged this. That while we used to pass down knowledge exclusively through our oral traditions, today we are doing it in new ways. One of those ways is through the written word.

I think there's value in our stories for others, but selfishly, I also don't want to lose the things I've known, experienced, researched, been told in the traditions we used to hold close in the development of our many cultures as Indigenous People. I want to document these things for myself so that when I forget, when memories break down over time, I can come here and renew them. And I want them for my family. For my parents, my brothers, their children, and mine. Because just as there are within these pages parts of who I am, there are parts of who they are, who they have been, and who they will become. This story will protect the memories I have of Dad.

One by one.

Moment by moment.

Memory by memory.

WE'RE DRIVING TO The Pas in a rented car in 2007. I have a captive audience for six hours, and I use it, asking Dad questions like I've done for years. I never wonder if he's getting tired of it, because he never looks like he is. We stay at the Kikiwak Inn in Opaskwayak Cree Nation for the two days we're there. I interview people in The Pas, conducting research for my graphic novel about Helen Betty Osborne. Dad comes with me to some of these interviews, stays back at the hotel for some, and finds his way to the gaming centre for others. I meet him there one night and try blackjack at a table for the first time. I lose twenty dollars faster than I can believe.

Before moving on to Cross Lake and Norway House, we drive out to Clearwater Lake, to the pump house where Betty was murdered. There's a memorial for her there, a white wooden cross with her name spelled out with nails. At the base of the cross, people have left things for her. Sweetgrass. Cigarettes. Money. Blankets, in case she gets cold out here in the winter, because she was cold out here the night she was murdered. Sage. Stuffed animals. I walk up to the cross, lean towards it, and place a pen on one of the arms. Dad and I stand before it and close our eyes. To our right is the lake, vast and beautiful and silent in the moment. Offering the calm and serenity that Dad's spoken about. A breeze brushes against my skin, shy and cool.

I had a nervous breakdown in the summer of 2010. There were so many changes in such a short span of time, and my body, my mind, gave out. We'd moved in April. I'd switched jobs in May. Lauren was born in June. Grandma Eyers died in July. I'd always held things in, pushed them down, but you can keep only so many things that deep. There is only so much space. I started to feel it in Melita, at Grandma Eyers's funeral. Something wasn't right. At the cemetery, where Grandma had already added her name to the headstone beside Grandpa's, I crouched down and put my hand on her urn. I stood up, and Cam and Mike were there. We hugged, and for the first time since her death, I cried. Later that month, I was playing ultimate frisbee when I started to feel off, like I had the flu. I got home and found Jill in our bedroom. I lay down on the bed and told her I wasn't feeling well. A week later, I stopped at Shoppers Drug Mart on the way home from work and tested my blood pressure. It was through the roof. When I got home, I called Health Links, and the person I spoke to told me to call an ambulance. Jill's at my bedside at Victoria General Hospital. I'm where Dad was nine years earlier. I think about that. They're testing to see if I'm having a heart attack, but they know I'm not. Mom and Dad arrive. My brothers. Dad stands at the foot of my bed, squeezes my toes. The doctor gives me Ativan.

It gets worse. I spend time in bed. I don't believe I have anxiety. I make appointments with doctors, with a lady somewhere in rural Manitoba who'll inspect my blood like she's reading tarot cards. My doctor gives me a prescription for anti-anxiety medication, a yellow plastic bottle with a white childproof lid. It's filled with little blue pills. Dad sits down beside me on the bed. I'm lying down. I'm always lying down. I start to cry. I'm sobbing. I can hardly talk. I tell him that I can't even walk down the hallway to go to the bathroom without feeling like I'm going to fall over. He listens to me. He talks to me. He opens the pill bottle, takes out one of the blue pills, and places it on my tongue.

We drive to Minnesota in 2014. My cousin Niigaan has lined me up to speak at the Native American Literature Symposium at Mystic Lake Casino Hotel. We arrive in the late afternoon, just before supper. I'm speaking tomorrow. There's less and less Dad can eat without stomach trouble. I shop for us at an organic grocery store close by. Pick up things I know Dad can eat. He stays behind in the hotel. I get back ready to eat with him, but he's gone. It's after eight now. I walk through the entire casino floor. The electronic beeps, the foot traffic, the flashing lights—all feed my anxiety. I find Dad tucked away in the corner, playing slots. I'm angry and relieved. He comes back to our hotel room an hour later. We eat together.

THE FIRST PICTURE book I wrote, *When We Were Alone*, arrives at my house in a cardboard box in December 2016. I cut the tape with a box cutter, open the lid, and pull out a copy. I look at the cover. Two girls are lying on their stomachs in a pile of autumn leaves. They are on the grounds of a residential school. They are smiling because they're together. When I tuck Lauren into bed that night, we read the book together. It's about identity. About how we learn from our grandparents and family, how we express ourselves through our clothing and hair, how language connects us to culture. And what happens when these things are denied us. When we finish, Lauren is thoughtful. I kiss her goodnight.

It's the next day. We're having our family over for brunch. My brothers and sisters-in-law, nieces and nephews, brother-in-law, parents-in-law, Mom and Dad. We have a dining room table that pulls out to stretch from wall to wall. There'll be almost thirty people over soon. The house is warm and smells like food. Jill's been cooking since early in the morning. Mom and Dad arrive first. Dad sits down at the table and is greeted immediately by Lauren. She jumps into his lap. He gives her a hug, and she disappears into his arms. When she reappears, she puts her hand against his cheek.

"Grandpa?" she says.

"Yes, my girl," he says.

"Will you teach me Cree?" she asks.

I understand intergenerational healing.

Another time, Lauren and I are at her grandma and grandpa's house. Grandpa is sitting in a chair by the window, almost exactly where Mom was sitting when I ran to her as a child. Lauren is standing in front of him, facing me. He has his hands on her shoulders. Lauren has asked me to sit on the love seat, to watch and listen. I've come to pick her up after work. Grandpa has been teaching her Cree.

"Tansi, Moshom." Hello, Grandpa.

"Kisākihitin." I love you.

"Okay, I'm going to say *api*."

"Api," Lauren repeats.

Grandpa says it one more time, and Lauren repeats him again.

"That means sit down," he says. "So I say *api* and you sit down."

"Okay, Moshom."

"Api, Lauren."

Lauren backs up and sits down on Grandpa's left knee, and he embraces her, wraps his arms around her. She and her light brown hair, grey sweats, socks turned the wrong way on her feet blends into my father's navy slacks and cardigan sweater, his salt-and-pepper hair. Her socks brush up against his bear claw moccasins.

"And then you say, when you want to stand up, *nipawi*."

"Nīpawi," Lauren says, and she bounces to her feet.

She sits down and stands up a few more times, then Grandpa stands beside her.

"Watch me," he says.

He starts to walk very slowly.

"Pimohtē," he says.

She walks with him.

"Pimohtē," she repeats.

They walk together across the living room to the kitchen, then turn around and come back. Dad sits down and has Lauren stand in front of him, facing him. They go over the words again.

"Api."

She sits criss-cross applesauce on the hardwood floor.

"Nīpawi."

She jumps up to her feet.

"Pimohtē."

She hesitates. Grandpa waits. I wait. She tilts her head thoughtfully for a moment, then walks in a tiny circle.

We both applaud, tell her, "Ekosi! Way to go!"

She spins while she walks.

"Is that enough, or do you want to learn more?"

"More."

We spend another twenty minutes together in my parents' living room. Grandpa says a word, then acts it out for her. Lauren repeats the word, then acts it out with an almost indescribable vivacity, the sort of energy that I haven't seen many people muster. But then, Grandpa tells her to watch him. He lines her up beside him, and for the first time in years, Dad jogs. He takes a lap around the living room. He's acting out the word *pimpahta*, "run." Lauren sprints back and forth when he says the word, her light brown hair flowing behind her as though she's swimming underwater.

This lesson between Lauren and her grandfather has animated Dad. It seems as though each day, he's getting thinner. Each day, weaker. The last time I saw him quicken his pace was a year earlier, at a golf tournament where he, Cam, Mike, and I were playing best ball. On the last hole, after teeing off, he tried to run off the tee box. I had to stop him from falling. It was another landmark of his age. With Lauren, teaching her Cree, he's energized in a way I won't see for another year, when Dad and I go to Black Water.

"What do you regret most?"

"That I didn't teach you the language."

I can hear him say it. He had his reasons, even if they turned out to be wrong. He had his reasons, but later in life, he realized the impact. I have come to understand the impact of that decision as well. I never learned to speak Cree, and as a consequence, my children have not learned either. As I watch Lauren spinning, jumping into Grandpa's lap, walking beside him, running to the kitchen and back, everything may change. *Api. Nīpawi. Pimohtē. Pimpahta.* We run away from what might have been towards what is now to come. Lauren has told me and Jill, on several occasions, that she plans to have an inordinate number of children. She may not have twenty, but she'll have a few. She will learn Cree. She will teach her children Cree. This is how we will heal. Intergenerational trauma requires this kind of act, purposefully working towards healing through the connections we choose to foster, the things we seek to learn, in whichever way we choose to learn them. But typically, this acquisition of knowledge, this learning, happens through Elders, happens through stories, and happens through the language.

Tansi, Moshom.

Kisākihitin.

I'M IN OTTAWA for the Governor General's Literary Awards celebration in November 2017. *When We Were Alone* has won for Young People's Literature—Illustrated Books. Jill can't stand going to fancy events or socializing much—she's an introvert—and declined to come with me. But I think it was something else too; I think that as much as she knew I wanted her to come, she also knew how important it was for my parents to be there. When I first knew that I wanted to be a writer, in the third grade, it was Mom I told, bursting into the house with *The Bestest Poems I've Ever Sawed* clutched proudly in my hand. When I decided that I was going to write books about Indigenous People, cultures, histories, communities, it was not only because of what I'd missed as a child but because of what I'd learned from Dad. About his life and the teachings he'd gifted me with. When I decided to write *When We Were Alone*, it was Nana I thought of. What she may have gone through, how she held on to herself despite the experience. I thought of Nana, I thought of my friend Betty Ross, I thought of Helen Betty Osborne. I thought of the thousands upon thousands of children who attended residential schools, the generations that had come after them, and those yet to come.

Mom and Dad make fast friends with several of the winners and their guests. They love Richard Harrison and Hiro Kanagawa. By the end of the first day, they're ready to adopt Julie Flett. And when I bump into Cherie Dimaline months later in Brampton at the FOLD literary festival, she tells me that she wanted to sit by my father all the time because there was a calmness to him that she felt drawn to.

On the second day, we load onto a tour bus and are taken to Parliament Hill. We'll tour the Library of Parliament, be recognized and applauded during Question Period, attend a reception with the Parliamentary Librarian and the Speaker of the House of Commons. The bus takes us to the front of the Centre Block, and we unload. We stand outside for a moment before entering the building. It's a sunny day but cool, and a breeze welcomes our arrival. Julie's been taking pictures all week. At one point, I'm standing just behind Dad, and she takes one of us. I don't see it at the time, but later, she shows me the photograph. Dad's wearing a light blue dress shirt underneath a V-neck sweater. A black coat and a scarf. I've got a grey motif going on. Dad's in the foreground, on the right side of the picture, looking somewhere off in the distance, to the left. I'm in the background, on the left side of the picture, looking somewhere ahead, to the right. Dad's shadow is resting against me, across half my body.

I JUMP IN my office chair, startled. Dad's rapped on my window with his cane. I look up, see him, and smile. I slip off my own bear claw moccasins, put on my shoes, and meet him at the front door. We greet each other with a hug. We walk together the short distance to the café, a place we've gone to for a visit countless times before. He orders tea, I order decaf coffee, and we sit in the same place we always do. Dad's facing the café, while I'm facing him and a mirror, and I trade glances between him and my reflection. I take a sip of coffee, then place it back onto the table delicately. We meet eyes. There's four feet of air between us; I've never felt closer to Dad than I do now. He's blindly playing with the lid of his tea, then leans forward the shortest distance.

"I want to go to my trapline one last time," he says.

Those words, in that moment, feel like the only sound in the world.

"Okay," I say. "Let's go."

THE BOAT SLIDES over the line, onto Black Water, and continues until the hull scratches against rocks on the shore. The surface is blanketed with loose rounded stones and slopes up towards the clearing. Dad digs his walking stick into the ground, and it secures itself between two stones. Another step. We're closer still. Just before he puts a foot onto the grass, I glance back and see more than just the space between here and the boat, the steps we've taken over that distance. I see my path and his, apart at first, then how they intersect. How our footprints lead from the boat, up the shoreline, to where we are now. Over the loose rounded stones, over the flat rocks of the Boreal Shield, over the path that leads between spruce trees, between bush and long grass. Over all this to Black Water, the open field where Dad used to live as a child, a place he's not been for seventy years but remembers the same way I do. In memories. In moments that will never fade because he's passed them on through the stories he's shared. His foot hovers over the grass for a moment, then he's home. The next moment, so am I.

MITATAHT-NIYANANOSAP
(FIFTEEN)

Dad walks ahead, supported by the stick his old trapline provided. I hang back with Eric, walk slower, watch Dad make
his way to the boulder in the middle of the clearing, the landmark
that signalled our arrival. Dad seems stronger, sturdier. I don't
feel the need to put my hand around his bicep, to support him
in any way, other than just to be here with him. He has the walking stick. He has Black Water. I know what I'm watching, the
significance of it. I look back towards the boat, at the footprints
we've left in our wake. I look at Dad, then ahead of him, where
footprints have not yet been made. A blank slate. A story yet to
be written.

There were three or four families that stayed here, Dad tells
me when he gets to the rock. He has his hand on the stone. They
stayed in tents, encircling the stone, this community of people.

This gathering place. From here, they would branch off, go their separate ways for the winter, and come back again when the frozen waters broke. From here, they would head back to Norway House, where their families and friends would be waiting along the shore, ready to welcome them home.

Dad looks around the land, full circle. He takes inventory of the area as though the things that used to be here are here still. He does this quietly first, breathing the memories in like air. The kind of air you can find only out here, clean and crisp, like the countless stars at night. I am quiet, watching him. Eric's quiet at my side. The land is quiet. I feel the calm that Dad has spoken about. Finally, he looks at me, and this welcomes me to join him. I approach the stone and lean against it. He looks around the land again, full circle. This time, as he turns, slow and methodical, a minute hand on a clock, he tells me about what he saw just moments earlier. The memories that he breathed in.

He points to the trees. The birch trees, the spruce trees, the jack pines. He tells us that a mile inland, there's a small lake. As a child, he used to swim there and walk around it just to spend time with the water. He says that he wishes he could go there now, but he can't. It would be too difficult at his age. For a moment, the weight of this rests heavily on my body and spirit. Here we are, on Black Water, where he used to live as a child, but there are places that we cannot go. Then I look into his eyes, see how he looks through the trees, and I know that he's gone there anyway. I can see the lake in his eyes. I can see him swimming in it. I can see him walking around it, skipping rocks over its surface, touching his toes against the cool water.

He shows me where the tents used to be, and where he did his chores. Into the trees, where he gathered the spruce boughs on which his family used to rest. He shows me an old pile of wood laid against the treeline, where he used to chop logs when he was old enough to use an axe. He shows me the water over there, over there, the different places where they'd set traps for muskrats. He shows me where they did the laundry and ate their meals—the mundane, everyday occurrences that he may have taken for granted at the time. They feel significant now, seminal moments in his life. Each moment is blood flowing through his veins.

The grass is shorter this time of year. We tour the area, visiting all the spots he can get to safely. The spots he showed me from the boulder and its shiny black surface—the trees, the woodpile, the water, where the tents used to be, where they ate food and did laundry. I try to picture him seventy years ago. He would've been here as a four-year-old, the same age as James, my youngest boy. He would've been here as a nine-year-old, the same age as Lauren, my youngest girl. At Lauren's age, he was expected to do more for his family. He was given his first trap to set. He remembers more when we come to different areas of Black Water. Little memories. Sometimes he tells us. There are depressions in the earth in one spot, a couple of them, side by side. This is where they used to store food. Other times, he keeps the memories to himself. He stops, falls silent, and I wait.

I don't know how long we stay on the land. I never think to check the time on my phone. I never think to listen for the rattle of pills in my pocket. There's no service out here. There's no time out here. Dad and I are catching a plane back to the city later in the day. I don't think about the plane or the city. When we decide to leave, we stand at the rock, side by side, and look out over the land and the water. It's quiet. We don't disrupt the calm. I see the boat. There's a path laid out before me. It leads from the boat to here. The trees open up to allow this journey. The bush opens up to allow this journey.

There's a path laid out before us. There is at first one set of footprints on the path, then two, far apart from each other. One closer to the water, the other closer to the forest. But slowly, assuredly, they come together until they're side by side. They continue on in this way. They reach the boulder and its smooth black surface. They stop where Dad and I are standing. When they were apart and when they came together, they were always leading here. I know it then. I can see it. I understand it as well as I understand myself. Everything Dad was, everything he is, is the journey that led here. Everything I was, everything I am, is the journey that led here, to Black Water.

We return to the boat and drift out onto the water, to where the water changes colour right in front of our eyes. From the Cambridge Blue we travelled on to get here to a deep and dark shade of midnight. We stop right on the line, and Eric has me drop the anchor. He hands me a fishing rod, gives another one to Dad, and keeps one for himself. We cast our lines into the water.

When I was younger, Mom took us boys on a trip down into the States, then up through Ontario. We camped all the way. At one stop, there was a man-made pond, a place where you were guaranteed to catch a fish. I was Lauren's age. As promised, each one of us returned to our campsite that evening with a fish. Mine seemed enormous, but on careful review of the pictures, I was just little and it made the fish look big.

You're not guaranteed to catch a fish on Black Water. When Dad was a child, if you were hungry, you had to catch something. A muskrat. A fish. If you didn't, you'd go hungry.

We fish for an hour or two before heading back to Norway House. In that time, Eric catches seven fish. It seems like he pulls one into the boat every minute, one after the other. Dad catches one fish. It fights with him, but he gets it into the boat and places it beside Eric's pile. There is one fish that is screwing with me. I bait my hook and cast into the water. I feel a nibble and probably get a little too excited. I reel in the line, but the frozen minnow is gone. One time, I manage to get the fish out of the water, but it jumps off the hook. I do not catch a fish.

In 2000, when I stepped out of the van and put a foot onto the ground in Norway House, a feeling came over me that I'd come home. It was a feeling I now recognize as blood memory—that the memories and lives of my ancestors, of Dad, are woven into the fabric of my DNA. That everything they lived through, everything they experienced, lives within me. I feel the same thing here, on Black Water. And sure, if I were living out here, if I were hungry and had to catch something, I'd probably starve. But as long as Dad and I have been talking, as much as I have learned about him—and by association about myself—I know that our journey isn't over. There is so much more for me to know. As the boat pulls away from the trapline and the black water churns behind us, I know that I'll come home again.

"Are you happy we went?" I ask over the boat's engine as Black Water disappears behind us.

"Yes," Dad says. "I still don't remember everything about the area, but I remember the country. It's so beautiful. I remember the water. It's like that, all the way. Water all over the place. When I miss it out here, I get homesick for the water."

Months later, sitting in my office, me in my chair and Dad on the couch, miles and miles away from the land, I ask him to describe what going to Black Water together meant to him.

"It was kind of sucky," he says, and chuckles.

I think, "Man, it would've been great if he'd said something incredibly poetic just then."

I wonder if that's all he's going to say, which wouldn't be outside the realm of possibility. When I call him, sometimes our conversations aren't many more words than that. He's more of an in-person talker. I stay patient. I stay calm. After a minute, he continues.

"You could feel the emotion. We started at the falls. That's eighteen miles from Norway House. There's a lot of land we didn't see, but at the same time, there was land that we saw. The memories that came back were emotional for me because I hadn't been out to Black Water for a long time." He stares out the window like we're there again, like he's looking all around the land. "And the changes. The changes. I don't remember all that swift water. I don't know if it was there before. I didn't know you had to go a certain way. You just paddled and rowed, and you got to there. You got home. It was a very emotional experience, a positive emotional experience. Because you could see how you learned. You could see the water, the trees, the birds, the sky, and you remember: they used to teach me about these things."

THE PAST FEW years, my family's been going on road trips. Four years ago, we headed west, camped all the way, and ended up on the northern tip of Haida Gwaii. We stayed in a cabin on the beach facing the Pacific Ocean. We were without running water, electricity, and cell service for days. The world could've been ending, and we wouldn't have known. On the morning we left, I stood on the beach with my feet in the water and felt the same kind of calm I would experience on Black Water. There was just the ocean, everywhere I looked, and the sound of waves. The journey took three weeks, and we ended our vacation in Clear

Lake. In 2018, we went in the opposite direction, driving through Ontario, Quebec, New Brunswick, and Prince Edward Island to get to Nova Scotia, where we stayed in a cabin near the Cabot Trail for three days. This year, we decided to head north, first to Norway House, then to Churchill.

When I first visited Norway House in 2000, I was twenty-three years old. I had these pictures in my head of what a reserve would look like, none of which matched up with reality. My kids are sixteen, thirteen, eleven, nine, and four. They all have a better idea at their age than I did at mine. This is not an indictment; it's to say a few things. One, I've been a consistent presence in their lives. I have always been there. I'd like to think I've had the sort of influence on my children's lives that my father wanted to have on mine. As he had on mine later in my life. They know what I do in my day job; they know what books I've written, and why I write them. Two, Jill and I have made a point of exposing our kids to various Indigenous cultures in a number of ways— visiting communities (Norway House will not be the first reserve they've been to), attending events, spending time at my work, reading a ton of books by my friends and fellow writers. All this has helped them understand things about Indigenous People and their cultures, histories, traditions that I didn't when I was their age. Three, they are aware of their cultural makeup. They are Cree. They are Métis. They are Scottish. They are English. They are Irish. They have been given the tools—the influence Jill and I have had on them, the exposure to knowledge that we have fostered in our home, the understanding of their cultural makeup—to figure out who they are, to be proud of who they are, and to know that they don't have to be the same as everyone else. What it means for my daughter Emily to be Indigenous will be different than what it means for Cole, Anna, Lauren, and

James. And their indigeneity will change as they grow older, as they learn new things, as they and I carry on a conversation that I hope lasts for decades.

While I believe this conversation has started already—and I know Jill and I have been teaching them about and exposing them to things that will help them on their journey—there is more we need to do, more places we need to go.

We're in one of those places now. Dad and Mom were supposed to come with us. It's impossible to predict these days when Dad will feel good and when he won't. But this week he's been unwell, and Mom felt it was better for him to stay home. I told him I'd take lots of pictures to show him upon our return to the city, and I will. I'll sit with him on his couch when we get back from Churchill and scroll through them with him, one by one, and tell him the story of our visit. We'll spend most of our time looking at the pictures from Black Water.

On the first full day in the community, I give my family a tour. I can do that now. I've spent enough time here. We visit the Fort and the parking lot across the street, where decades earlier Dad went to school. We track down my auntie Flora outside the mall and visit with her on a metal bench surrounded by community members and rez dogs. Lauren can't stop hugging her. Auntie Flora can't stop hugging Lauren. We drive along Jack River, where we can see across the water to Towers Island. I tell them about Nana and her siblings, about the day school that used to be there. We go to the old cemetery. I've not been able to find immediate family here on previous visits, but this time around I find Donald (Dulas) Alexander McIvor's grave. We stop in front of the church, and I tell my kids about the time their grandfather returned home after his years in Phoenix and tried to give a sermon in Cree.

The stories that I've learned, that Dad has told me, are stories I can tell my kids. They are stories my kids will tell their kids one day. As we drive to the West Island, to the cottage we're staying at for the three days we're here, I think about that. I think about it, and imagine them here with my grandkids. They tour them through the community because they can do that. They tell them stories about when their grandfather was younger, and about the trip they took with their dad. Isn't that, in the end, what this is all about?

We're on the water with Eric and his grandson, in two boats headed towards Black Water and, hopefully, the trapline that Dad lived on for two years. We pass Black Water for the moment and continue on for miles, all the way to Hairy Lake. It's difficult to boat through the reeds. The motor keeps getting stuck in them. But eventually, we make it all the way across, and we stop to eat on some flat rocks, on a trapline that used to be somebody else's.

"At the northeast corner of Hairy Lake, there's a narrow river that leads to the trapline," Dad told me last night when I asked how to get there. He sounded excited at the prospect, told me that the cottage they lived in might still be standing. "That river leads to another small lake. At the south shore is where we stayed."

I tell Eric. He knows the place. He knows, too, that we cannot make it there in the boats we're in. The passageway is too narrow. We'd need to get there in a canoe, in the way Dad and his family used to get there. I'll have to come back when I have more time and try to find it.

We head south across Hairy Lake towards Black Water. Before getting there, however, we stop on the water, throw our anchors, and fish. Each one of us gets a rod. Eric's brought James one that's blue, his favourite colour, and no longer than three feet. We cast our lines into the river and are overcome with the quiet, until the first fish is caught and cheers erupt from both boats.

The fish are biting. We spend three hours fishing, and by the time we pull up the anchors, there are thirty fish between the two boats. Everybody catches at least one, even James and Lauren. By some miracle, I catch five fish. If I were living on the land and was hungry, I wouldn't starve. I would have enough to feed my family. How much difference a year makes.

As the sun begins to fall and warm colours cast against the waters and the land, we arrive at Black Water. We pull the boats up to the shore and disembark. There is a path in front of us that leads to the black boulder in the middle of the clearing. The trees and bush open to allow our passage. The kids sit on the rock, and I stand in front of it. I take inventory of the land, looking all around it, full circle. I show them where the tents used to be, and the places where Dad used to do his chores. I point into the trees, where he gathered spruce boughs, and deeper in the forest, where there's a lake he used to swim in and walk around. The old pile of wood at the treeline where he used to chop logs when he was old enough to use an axe. I show them the water, the places where they set traps for muskrats. Where they did laundry, ate their meals. This was a gathering place for our family. Everything feels significant now. Seminal moments in the life of our family, the lives of those who came before us. Each moment is blood flowing through our veins.

On the way back to the boat, Lauren pulls on my arm. I stop where she is while the others walk towards the water. I kneel down so that we're at eye level. She looks around, full circle, then meets my eyes.

"I love it here," she says. "Everything is calm."

Nineteen years ago, I stepped out of a burgundy Dodge

Caravan and put my foot onto the ground in Norway House Cree Nation, and a feeling came over me. Lauren feels the same thing now. Blood memory. The memories and lives of our ancestors are woven into the fabric of her DNA. Everything they lived through, everything they experienced, lives within Dad, lives within me, lives within her. This is the way things have always been. This is the way things will always be.

EPILOGUE

━━━

My dad is in his early eighties, and despite my best efforts to will his immortality, he's not getting younger. He will not be a boy again. He will not be the father I used to know—the father I was unfamiliar with—again. Years from now, he will not be this father either. Years from now, he will exist in memories, and I will be left to collide with the open arms of those moments.

I remember writing those words no more than a year ago, after Dad and I had spent a week together. After we'd engaged in a marathon interview session that was as tiring for him as it was invigorating. On the Monday, he was cautious with his words. He was visibly guarded. By Friday, he couldn't say enough. He'd remember things and offer them up without hesitation, and I accepted these gifts. For the book, sure, but more importantly for myself, my children, his sons, his grandchildren, and generations yet to come. It was an exciting time, too, because it felt like the beginning of a new phase in our relationship. We'd been talking for years, yes, but not like this. These were the first words in an entirely new conversation, the first steps in a journey that I'd always hoped we'd take.

I thought that I had more time with Dad. I thought that we had years to talk. I thought that we had years to sit together on the couch in his basement and do nothing more than be together in the quiet. I thought that we had years to golf together, and that no matter how old he got, or how frail, he'd beat me. I thought that we had years to watch movies together at Grant Park Theatre, talking with each other until the house lights dimmed. I thought that we had years to sit by the fire outside of his cabin at Thunderbird Bungalows in Clear Lake with Mom and Cam and all our kids. I thought that we had years to meet for lunch at a place where we could both eat, because he has no large intestine and I'm vegan. I thought that we had years to meet at education conferences. I thought that we had years to sit together in his study and talk about everything that was going on with my work, with my writing, with my life. I thought that we had years. I thought that we had more time. But we didn't.

Dad passed away, suddenly but peacefully, on December 27, 2019.

His death has brought as many regrets about the times I could've talked to him, could've been with him, as it has regrets about the times we have lost, the times I so desperately wanted to have, and thought we would have.

On Boxing Day, I was driving out to Canmore with my family, and while we were still on the road, Jill called Mom. Dad answered. Jill asked for Mom. Dad called for her from the basement, then Mom was on the phone and Dad hung up. That was my last chance to talk to him. No more than a day later, just the blink of an eye in the span of a lifetime, I was on a plane back to Winnipeg to be with my brothers and Mom.

Jill and I alternate where we have Christmas dinner. One year we spend it with the Dumonts, one year with the Robertsons. In 2019, it was the Dumonts' turn. We stayed at Jill's parents' house until around 9:30 p.m. and then headed home. I knew that I wouldn't see Mom and Dad for about a week, and it was Christmas, so when we pulled into the driveway I almost told Jill I was going to pop by just to say hi to them. Almost. But we had to get up at 3:30 a.m. to start our drive to Canmore, and I didn't want to be up that late. I decided to stay home. I could've had one more hour with Dad. We could've shared some gluten-free snacks. We could've sat together on his couch and watched television. It wouldn't have mattered what show; it never did.

There are regrets that stretch far beyond the immediate past. A few years ago, I promised Dad that I'd go see a movie with him. I can't remember what movie it was; it doesn't matter anymore. Things came up, I couldn't go to the movie, and I forgot to tell Dad. The next day, Mom told me that he'd waited for me to pick him up. He'd sat on his chair and watched out the window for my car to pull up to the curb, but I never came. It would've been three more hours spent with him that I'll never have. A drive to the movie theatre and back. A conversation in two comfortable chairs, side by side, before the house lights dimmed. Two hours beside him.

On January 2, 2020, I met Mom and Cam at the funeral home. Dad had to be identified before the cremation. I went to support Mom and Cam, who were going to view Dad's body, and I'd been waffling for days. I wanted to see him. I didn't want to see him. Both Cam and Mom thought I shouldn't, but they told me that it was my choice. Both Cam and Mom told me that he wasn't there anymore. It wasn't really him. He was gone.

Two days before Christmas, Jill and I drove over to Mom and Dad's house in River Heights to give them their presents. Dad was in the basement. I went down to give him his gift: a framed photograph of him, me, Mike, Cam, Elijah, and Mom that I took with my cellphone after the Winnipeg Blue Bombers won the Grey Cup on November 24, 2019. I'd propped my phone up against the bottom corner of the television, set a ten-second timer, and run behind the couch, behind Dad, and the picture somehow turned out perfectly.

I told Dad to open his present even though it was two days early, because I might not see him on Christmas Day. He did, and then we sat together on the couch, on the star blanket he'd been given years earlier. There was a football game on: the Giants versus the Redskins. I told Dad how much I hated that so many sports teams still had racist names and mascots. He got annoyed at me.

"Aren't there more important things to worry about in the world right now?" he asked.

I backed down. I told him there were. I didn't want him to be annoyed at me, and besides, he was right. There were more important things to worry about. There are.

The game went into overtime. I put my head on Dad's shoulder. At some point, I fell asleep, just for a few minutes. I never fall asleep watching television. I have trouble falling asleep, period. My brain doesn't shut off. That's why I have anxiety. That's why I take medication. But I didn't need it that night. Not with Dad beside me. Not with his arm pressed up against mine. He was my calm. I'll feel that sort of calm again only when I return to Black Water, because Dad will be with me there too.

At some point, I woke up. Dad turned his head to look at me. After the game ended, Jill called down the stairs that it was time to go. I stood up, leaned over, and kissed him on the top of his head. That was the last time I saw him. That will always be the last time I saw him. He exists now only in memories, and I am left to collide with the open arms of those moments.

Kisākihitin, Dad. Travel well.

DONALD (DULAS) ALEXANDER ROBERTSON

MAY 18, 1935–DECEMBER 27, 2019

ACKNOWLEDGEMENTS

———

There are so many people who helped me write this book, by taking the time to talk with me, provide research material, uncover records, spend the day out on the land with me and my father, message with me, talk with me on a bus ride at a writer's festival, and so on.

First and foremost, I want to acknowledge my father, Donald Alexander Robertson. In many ways, we were working on this story together for decades. But in the final two years of his life, he spent so much time with me, including a marathon week that I know tired him out, as much as he loved the experience. "Are you getting what you need?" he asked more than once. Yes, Dad. I got what I needed. I got time with you that I'll never forget. I got your voice on a recorder that I can listen to for the rest of my life. *Kisākihitin.*

The rest of my family was there with me every step of the way, whether they spoke with me for the book or not. My mother, Bev

273

Robertson, supported me just as she always has, even during the very hard last months, when we lost my dad and her husband. You are my hero, Mom. My brothers have always been there for me when I've needed them. *Ekosani*. My sisters-in-law, brothers-in-law, father- and mother-in-law, OGG. Thank you. I have five children—Emily, Cole, Anna, Lauren, and James—and in many ways, I wrote this book for them, so that one day it might help them discover a piece of who they are. And so they'd know their grandfather a bit better than they had before. I love you, kids. My wife, Jill, who does all the hard, thankless work so that I can write books, who keeps me on my feet when I'm about to fall—words aren't enough.

I would like to acknowledge Library and Archives Canada, the National Centre for Truth and Reconciliation, the Selkirk Mental Health Centre, the CBC, the University of Winnipeg, the University of Manitoba, the United Church of Canada, the Winnipeg Arts Council, Norway House Cree Nation, HarperCollins, and the Manitoba First Nations Education Resource Centre.

Special thanks to Strini Reddy, Amanda Tetrault, Aunties Marion and Effie, Cousins Tammy and Olive and Shayne, Uncle Robert, Jim Gifford, Jennifer Lambert, Noelle Zitzer, Janice Weaver, Chris Kelly, Susan Wingert, Nicole Magne, Amber Green, Jen Storm, Ryan Johnston, Eric Ross, Darlene Osborne, Kathleen McCandless, Jackie Kaiser, Rachel Giese, Alice Kuipers, Wab Kinew, Jaclyn Hodsdon, David G. Williamson, Lorne Keeper, Scott B. Henderson and anyone else I may have forgotten. *Ekosani*. Thank you for everything.